THE AMBER TRAIL

By the same author

AN AMAZON AND A DONKEY

THE
AMBER TRAIL

A JOURNEY OF DISCOVERY
BY BICYCLE, FROM THE
BALTIC SEA TO THE AEGEAN

NATASCHA SCOTT-STOKES

WEIDENFELD & NICOLSON
LONDON

First published in 1993 by Weidenfeld & Nicolson,
an imprint of the Orion Publishing Group, Orion House,
5 Upper Saint Martin's Lane, London WC2H 9EA

A catalogue record for this book is available from
the British Library

ISBN 0 297 81306 4

Printed in Great Britain by
The Bath Press, Avon

Map of Poland from *Heart of Europe* by Norman Davies,
reproduced by kind permission of Oxford University Press;
maps of Hungary from *A History of Hungary* by P.F.Sugar et al.,
reproduced by kind permission of I.B.Tauris & Co.

Contents

MAPS

ACKNOWLEDGEMENTS

Thanks to Anthony Cheetham and Ion Trewin for giving me a chance.

For help and advice in England thanks go to Catherine Rosenberg of PEN; Sue Hall of Cycle Touring and Campaigning (CT&C); Arthur Defries; Ilona Stariczack; Lesley Pitman, Assistant Librarian of the School of Slavonic and East European Studies (SSEES); the following academic staff at SSEES: S. Eile, B. M. Mazur, V. Swoboda, P. J. S. Duncan, M. Bojcun, N. Davies, and most especially Dr Frank Carter; and Professor Lord Renfrew of Kaimsthorn, University of Cambridge.

Thanks also to Walter J. Jeffrey, the late General Secretary of the Writers' Guild of Great Britain; B. M. Ager, Curator of the Department of Medieval and Later Antiquities at the British Museum; the staff at the Expedition Advisory Centre of the Royal Geographical Society; Pete and Clare Openshaw; Steve of Chamberlain's bike shop, London; Rachel Charles for research on British media coverage of Serbia; Susannah Tarbush; and last, but not least, Martin Hohenleutner for finding obscure texts.

For help or hospitality during the journey, I would like to thank Juliusz and Zofia Kalert; Darek Balicki; Dorota; Mr Iglikowski; Mr Imre Szász and his colleagues; Alexander; Mr Bogdanović and his colleagues; Jovan and family; Aleksa and family.

And most of all, thanks to Benoît LeBlanc for everything from research on amber and bikes, to navigating, companionship and positive criticism. For useful comments on the text, my thanks, as always, to Charity Scott-Stokes, as well as to Christopher Portway, Elsbeth Lindner and Ion Trewin. Lastly, thanks to the copyright holders for kind permission to use the quotes heading each country section.

The Amber Trail

INSPIRATIONS

In October 1989 I was resting in Huaraz/Peru. I had just completed the most important challenge of my life: to travel the length of the Amazon, from its Marañón source to the Atlantic off Brazil, and now I was back where I had first set off, enjoying the Andean mountains I had come to love. Resting here, I read voraciously. Anything I could find in the English language was welcome after months of travelling in Latin America, and I read all the mouldy old paperbacks gathering dust at the guest house.

One of these was a historical novel by James A. Michener called *Poland*. It was overlong and, I admit, I skipped some pages. But at the back I found a map that caught my eye. It showed Eastern Europe and the changing borders of historic Poland and, among many others, there was a dotted line that meandered from the port of Gdańsk south, eventually heading east into the Ukraine and ending at Odessa on the Black Sea. I remember thinking that it seemed to suggest an interesting route for a journey in that part of the world, and then thought no more about it.

A month later, back in London, the Berlin Wall came down on 9 November and I spent the entire weekend in a state of shock. It was an event that touched me most personally, in a way I would never have imagined. It was extraordinary. But the fact that the Wall was being broken and the division of Germany was no more hit me at a deep emotional level I could only vaguely understand. Yet the sensations were forcing themselves on me with such urgency that I could think of nothing else. I perturbed my friends that weekend, and departed with a preoccupied look on my face, insisting on going home instead of lounging around with them.

What did it have to do with me? I was born of Anglo-German parents in 1962, a year after the Berlin Wall was built and, for me, Germany was always West Germany. The country to the east was an alien place, unseen, but somehow threatening. Without ever hearing anything much about East Germany, growing up in Munich I subconsciously developed an inbuilt fear of that 'other place'. The land on the opposite side of killer guards and barbed wire and land-mines. A place where people were supposed to have no proper clothes or fresh food. Where people queued for everything all the time and where you had to watch what you said in case someone from the Party was listening. One of my German aunts is from 'over there', and in my child's mind I remember an eerie sense of her otherness, like a terminally ill person who shows no symptoms.

I left Germany in 1979, deciding to reject my German heritage and become English. I had always spoken both languages, so on the surface at least there was no difficulty about emigrating to the other side of the Channel. I was sick of the gross materialism of culture in Munich, of the judgemental clamp of conformity that tried to squeeze life out of anyone who was different: anyone who laughed too loud on trains, didn't dress respectably, or walked barefoot on summer streets.

It seemed to me too, at the time, that Germany had come intolerably close to being a police state. The official response to the Baader–Meinhof gang and others like them was very repressive. Stop-and-search scenes were commonplace. So was being filmed by security agents at rock concerts and demonstrations. *Berufsverbot* was the spectre hovering over intellectuals who dared to speak out for leftist reforms, which branded them as communists whether they were or not. The right to privacy and freedom of opinion seemed to be crumbling ever more and I decided this was a country I no longer wished to live in.

But being in England has not always been a happy experience either. As a child I went briefly to an English boarding school and that was the first time I was confronted with the fact that I am half-German. 'I bet your dad's a Nazi,' they would say, and call me 'Hitler' instead of by my name. At the age of eleven I was suddenly bombarded with horror stories of the Second World War, of Jews' skins being turned into lampshades or bodies melted down for soap.

At the time I was helpless against the cruelties of my schoolmates. I tried to explain that my father was only a child in 1939, that my German grandfather had never been a member of the Nazi Party nor fought in the war. All that was irrelevant. To them I was a Kraut who came from a country where they shouted *Sieg Heil*. They had seen it on the television and in their comics, and their parents had never tried to tell them anything different. When my mother complained to the headmistress she was told that racism and nationalist bullying did not occur at her school. We were in England where we don't have that kind of thing.

The result of those early taunts was that I grew up with a horror of anything to do with the Second World War, blocking it out so that even the starting and finishing dates are quite recent knowledge for me. The memories were too painful, and whenever I did see images of piled-up corpses on old news reels, I always found myself with a very emotional response. Tears were always close although, beyond the obvious horror, I was never quite sure why. What has it got to do with me that in a time before I was born there were atrocities in the land of my birth? I wasn't even the first generation after the war. And yet the sense of shame and sorrow was always there, an awful and undeniable part of my personal heritage.

Over the next two years I was preoccupied with other things. I had been at a loose end after returning from Peru, and I accepted a contract that took me to Central America. It seemed like a good idea at the time, taking me back to one of my favourite parts of the world. Yet I followed developments in Europe with interest, and the dotted line through Eastern Europe I had seen in Michener's *Poland* book repeatedly drew my thoughts in that direction. Apparently the line marked a trade route for amber, and the idea of it increasingly caught my imagination. Wouldn't it be fun to cycle from the Baltic to the Black Sea . . . I liked the sound of it, and gradually the idea for a journey crystallised.

I wanted to travel slowly, close to the land and the people. But having just walked about one thousand kilometres through the Peruvian Andes, I'd had enough of travelling on foot to last me a long time. A bicycle seemed like the next best option, which would still provide enough flexibility to stop off any time, and freedom to follow country paths if I pleased. Most importantly of all, being on a bicycle would pose no threat or disturbance, nor cut me off from others.

It would be an excellent opportunity to discover a part of Europe I did not know, yet which was very close. It would also be a long-overdue positive response to my childhood experiences of prejudice and impotent rage, to the uncomfortable fact of having grown up half-English and half-German, two cultures congenitally at odds with each other, and a chance to bring substance to the faith I always clung to: that people are not so different, but only from other cultures, which there is no need to fear nor harbour prejudice about.

How would my own preconceptions match up against those of Poles or other Eastern Europeans? Is there anything in common between us, especially between people of my generation, children of the 1960s? Is there any sense in speaking of a New Europe? At the very least I could find out what the countries traced by the amber route looked like. And who could tell, perhaps there would be common ground too.

FALSE STARTS AND PREPARATION

So what exactly is amber? My earliest memory of it is a pendulous necklace worn by my grandmother. The large polished beads were a golden honey colour, and if you held them in your hand, they soon became warm and irresistibly malleable. Each segment glittered with mysterious fragments if caught in the light – bits of forest debris and even insects, I was told, millions of years old. Fly wings and beetle legs or even whole insects could be found entombed in amber, which was interesting for natural historians too, who had counted nearly two hundred different types of insects that must have existed all that time ago.

Amber is fossilised tree resin, which is indeed millions of years old, formed by the amber forests that once stood in the region now known as Finland, Scandinavia and the Baltic States.[1] Chemically speaking, it is classed as a non-metallic mineral, which belongs to the hydrocarbon group. In other words, it is a bitumen, similar to mineral pitch or gum copal. Unlike those, however, it has the interesting feature of being fluorescent, and also has a magnetic quality, which means if you rub amber on a surface, it then attracts light objects, such as hair or pine needles. These characteristics, as well as the gorgeous pine fragrance given off when amber is warmed, have fascinated people since earliest history. Occasionally this has been reflected in poetry, and a good example is Alexander Pope, born in the late seventeenth century, who wrote:

> Pretty! in amber to observe the forms
> Of hairs, or straws, or dirt, or grubs or worms!

[1] I am talking about Baltic amber, which accounts for approximately 88 per cent of the world's amber harvest. Very small amounts are also found in Romania, Sicily, Siberia, Burma, Greenland, Mexico, the Dominican Republic, the United States and the Anglian coast of Britain.

The things we know are neither rich nor rare,
But wonder how the devil they got there.
(From *An Epistle to Dr Arbuthnot*, 1. 169)

About forty to fifty million years ago, if you can imagine such time spans, amber pines (*Pinus succinifera*) covered a large area of land that was many times submerged and then lifted above sea level during the earth's youth. The trees and their resin, however, have long since disappeared under layers and layers of other land matter, or wash freely on the bottom of the Baltic Sea, where they have formed a reef of 'blue earth', which yields some of the best amber.

Occasionally autumn storms toss lumps of amber on to the beaches and, from time immemorial, the coastal inhabitants of the Baltic have combed their beaches for these treasured pieces. As early as the north European Bronze Age (1600–750 BC), amber was being carved into animal or mythical shapes, as well as into decorative beads, while some suggest that routes for exchange of copper, amber and gold were already established between cultures of the Baltic, Central Europe and the Aegean, by 3000 BC.

Most Baltic amber deposits, however, do not come from the sea, but are mined inland, and the regions that have traditionally yielded the most are the Jutland and Samland peninsulas, which roughly mark a coastal area stretching from Denmark to Lithuania – the south Baltic – with the largest deposits today on Polish and Lithuanian land.

Since there are no written records for prehistoric times, the earliest sources to be found on amber are from the Greeks and Romans, who valued it as an ornament and for the mystical powers they believed it held. In fact, the supernatural element shines through clearly in the Greek word for amber, which was *electron*, meaning 'substance of the sun', and the root from which we take our modern word 'electricity'. From earliest times it has been regarded as a source of benign power, with the ability to heal such diverse ailments as rheumatism, lung disease, toothache and throat infections; to protect against the evil eye; or to worship the sun.

According to Culpeper's *Dispensatory*, dated in 1654, amber was also supposed to help against diseases of the head, coughs, spitting of blood, nose bleeds, difficulty passing water, gonorrhoea and even hysteria. 'You may take ten or twenty grains at a time,' it says.

It is interesting to read the theories and legends Greek philosophers relate to the origin of amber. There is the story of the impetuous Phaethon, son of the god Helios, who took off with his father's chariot, careering around the skies so wildly that sparks from his wheels created the Milky Way, while a burning trail consumed portions of the earth. As punishment for upsetting the heavens, Zeus struck him down with a thunderbolt. His sisters rushed to the scene of his death and cried so uncontrollably that they metamorphosed into poplar trees. Once a year from then on, the trees 'cried' sap, which became what we know as amber.

The Roman, Pliny the Elder, had no time for poetic tales like this, and went into some detail to scoff at the Greeks in his *Natural History*. Demostratus comes in for particular ridicule for calling amber *lyncurion*, believing it came from lynx' urine. According to him, male urine produced the red and golden amber, while white and cloudy amber came from females. Nicias, on the other hand, preferred the idea that powerful rays of sunshine made the earth sweat, and it was these beads of moisture, washed away by the ocean's tide, that were later thrown up as amber on German coasts. Pliny is most scathing about Sophocles, who wrote that amber came from distant Indian birds that yearly wept tears for the death of the Greek, Meleager. What really bothered him was that a man of such 'elevated position' and 'high repute' should have displayed such contempt for mankind, 'to assert with impunity an intolerable falsehood'. He goes on to explain in suitably condescending tone that amber, of course, comes from resinous pine trees.

In defence of the Greeks it has to be said that the geographical location of the Baltic was not precisely known to them, nor was amber an important item of trade in the Classical Age, so why should they know where it came from? Not until the emergence of the Roman Empire did amber become a highly prized luxury in recorded history, and amber trade had its heyday from the first to fifth century. Only the Middle Ages saw the trade emerge once more, and from that time onwards it has steadily declined, amber no longer ranked equal with pearls by modern women. Roman ladies, on the other hand, were prepared to pay more for a fine amber carving than for a human slave in the prime of life.

The other source of information on amber comes from archaeologists, who have unearthed a great many amber artifacts which help to establish theories of early exchange of goods or migration routes. Not surprisingly, the most numerous and largest finds have been discovered along the southern Baltic. But from here, sumptuous graves and hordes of treasure have been found at regular enough intervals to indicate certain clearly established routes along which amber was carried to distant places. My research revealed that one of these followed the Polish Vistula and Ukrainian Dniester to the Black Sea, just as indicated in Michener's book, and I set about trying to find out more. Not only about historic amber either, but on any subject that remotely affected my proposed journey.

One of the first things I did was to look in the phonebook under 'P'. Quite unexpectedly I found almost two pages of organisations beginning with 'P' for Polish, and I wrote out all the addresses I thought might be useful, everyone from the Polish Embassy to the Polish Women's Association. Even more surprising to me was that under 'U' for Ukraine I found four addresses, and even an English language *Ukrainian Review*.

My next step was to go to the London School of Slavonic and East European Studies (SSEES) and find out where to learn Russian, and scan their prospectus for academic staff with specialist knowledge who could help me. The most important details I needed to know related to the exact route the amber used to take, so that I could study modern maps for the closest path to the historic one. I found a total of fourteen academic staff to write to – of which five wrote back within two months. Still, those that did reply all had very useful information to offer, often including daunting bibliographies for me to study.

I decided that Russian would be the most useful language in the circumstances, since I only had four months to prepare for the journey, and there was no way I could learn more than the basics of one language in that time. So even though the countries I was expecting to travel in used Polish and Ukrainian, it was going to have to be the old lingua franca of Eastern Europe: Russian. I would have to be careful to explain this later on, lest anyone took offence to the scorned imperial tongue. But a Ukrainian acquaintance assured me that people would be understanding, with one of his country's oldest jokes:

Q: What is the difference between a language and a dialect?

A: A language is a dialect with an army and a navy.

Finding somewhere to learn Russian was not so easy. Many courses were only running from the start of the academic year, in the autumn, yet

I needed somewhere that could begin teaching me in February and didn't charge too much money either. But after much phoning I found an excellent language centre at South Bank Polytechnic, and soon I was set up for my first tutorial.

'Excuse me,' I said, lost amongst the tangle of roads leading off Elephant and Castle roundabout. 'Can you tell me where London Road is? I'm looking for South Bank Polytechnic.'

'What part are you looking for?' asked the passer-by, a large man tightly packed into an overcoat, scarf wrapped up to his nose against the winter blasts.

'Well, the language centre,' I said hopefully, and to my amazement he told me that I must be his new Russian student, so we could go together. I was sure it was fate and a good omen, and I liked him already. Arthur was his name, and he strode off at a brisk march, which was just the style he liked to teach in too.

Russian is a strange code when you first see it, and to a newcomer its Cyrillic letters look completely unfamiliar. The first thing Arthur did was to read through the Russian alphabet, while I listened, trying to remember the new sounds. Straight away he wanted me to repeat the exercise on my own, but it was impossible. I couldn't even remember the fifth letter, let alone all thirty-two. How to remember what symbol meant which sound and how to pronounce it? Not only that. But the stress and pronunciation of the same letters could change depending on at least two options in any given word. After three weeks of intermittent study the only expression that stuck in my mind was the first I learnt: *Izvinitye pashalasta* (Excuse me, please).

Time was flying by and still I could not string a Russian sentence together, nor had I got very far with gathering information about the amber route. One source wrote '... at no time did I find amber of special interest during the medieval period' – which for some reason I thought was the relevant era.

In fact, it appeared that amber was much more important during prehistoric times and the main route for it was not from Poland to the Black Sea via the Ukraine, but south, across the Sudeten mountains, down the Danube to Belgrade, and thence to the Vardar–Morava valleys towards the Aegean Sea.

Perhaps that was just as well. War seemed to be imminent in Moldavia, through which I would have had to travel on my original route along the Dniester River to Odessa. And due to bureaucratic struggles between the old Russian order and the emergent Ukrainian and Moldavian ones, finding out who was responsible for entry visas had proved impenetrable: 'Just fly to Kiev and offer them US$60.' So much for good omens.

My new route would take me through Poland, Czecho-Slovakia, Hungary, Serbia and Macedonia: a journey of roughly 2,500 kilometres, from Gdańsk to Thessaloníki. It promised to be an exciting trip, covering almost all the Eastern European countries formerly locked in communism, and passing through a much greater variety of landscape and culture than my original route. I'd always wanted to go to Prague, and now I quite unexpectedly had my chance – not to mention visiting the ancient cities of Gdańsk, Kraków, Budapest and Belgrade ... This new turn to my project was a great boost and I couldn't wait to get going.

To be honest I was also relieved not to have to continue with learning Russian – in spite of the wasted time and money – because I obviously wasn't going to get very far in the couple of months left before I planned to set off. Instead I hoped that my German would be useful, even though I'd been told that some older Poles might not wish to speak it. (A suggestion I later found to be quite untrue.)

I wanted to leave at the beginning of June, by which time I expected the weather to be good and myself to have prepared as many aspects of the journey as possible. There was certainly a lot to be done: I still knew almost nothing about amber, let alone its historic role, and this quite apart from all the practical matters of preparation.

In the meantime, I also got married, and Benoît, who had been cycle touring before, announced that he wanted to come too. This was a nice idea, but it was also a nerve-racking one. How would I cope with travelling in company when I had always been a loner? Never, in fifteen years of travelling, had I ever wanted to be anything other than single. I relished the freedom and opportunities of solo travel, and never thought the occasional loneliness was too high a price for privacy and independent decision-making.

The possibility of making this journey together was emotionally attractive, but as a habitually independent person there were also doubts in my mind. What if he cramped my style or we got on each other's nerves?

What if being a couple stopped me from meeting interesting people? What if our pace did not match? Was it worth risking such a challenge to a relatively young relationship? Furthermore, was I not asking too much of myself, considering I had never wanted to have a companion before, to try it for the first time on a journey that was expected to take up to eight weeks? Most of all, I feared that travelling as a couple might dull my senses to experience, distract my attention from the finer details around me.

I already knew that Benoît's style of travel was not like mine, that although he enjoyed discovering new countries and cultures, he did not like roughing it, and camping, which is what I intended to do on this journey, was not his idea of fun at all. In fact, he told me he hated camping. Oh dear. Equally daunting was the thought that Benoît might subvert my decision-making, either by unwillingness, or favouring other options, or by myself becoming uncharacteristically docile and allowing him to take over what was actually my project. It was hard to resist selfish and possessive thoughts, and the only reason they failed to influence me is that I knew Benoît well enough by now to know he would *probably* do none of the things I naturally worried about.

Much as it went against my grain, I had to have faith in someone else. This was, after all, the man I had decided to share my life with, so I might as well start living up to my choice from the start. Never had I met a person easier to get on with, yet who did not let my Aries nature overpower him. I remember sharing this discovery with my mother, to which she replied. 'You must be compatible, dear.'

Tentatively I decided to give us both a chance and not prejudge the situation, but it was a big step for me to take, and added an extra worry to hover at the back of my mind. At least we could share the burden of preparation, and Benoît not only set to work finding out what kind of bicycle and equipment we should use, but also pre-read historical books and papers, marking all the relevant passages for me. What a luxury! An assistant, expedition partner and lover, all in one.

I concentrated on trying to match the ancient place names I found in obscure texts to ones I could find on a modern map. This was not always easy, since I not only had to find the equivalent for Latin place names, but also the Polish ones for places referred to by their former German names, or antiquated English names, if the author was from Britain. It took me some time to realise, for example, that the 'March river' was actually the Czecho-Slovak Morava, or that the Roman fort of Carnuntum was now the Austrian village of Petronell. It was a proper mystery tour trying to find each successive point for our amber trail.

What fun though to pour endlessly over maps of Eastern Europe and slowly trace a line that would take us from the Polish port of Gdańsk, southward past the Teutonic castles, along the Vistula, then south-west, through the ancient heart of Poland and medieval cities like Poznań (Posen) and Wrocław (Breslau); over the Kłodzko Pass (formerly the Glatz Pass) and into the Moravian plain of Czecho-Slovakia, until the Morava River would melt into the Danube outside the city of Bratislava.

Onwards along the Danube we'd go, crossing into Hungary and following the river to Budapest and all the way to Serbian Belgrade. Would there be war there by the time we arrived? There was no way of telling, but it added an extra *frisson* to our anticipation, and I boldly drew lines skirting into Romania and Bulgaria if we should have to divert.

'There's lots of mountains there you know,' Benoît tried to warn me.

'Oh, that's all right,' I breezed, 'we'll be fit by then.'

Rivers were to be our guide, and from Belgrade there would be two more to follow: first the Serbian Morava heading south towards the self-proclaimed Macedonian Republic and then, from its new capital of Skopje, we would trace the Vardar River through an ominously mountainous region before reaching the Macedonian plain of northern Greece.

The port of Thessaloníki was to be our final destination. It seemed like a good place to stop, though based on the records we could have travelled all the way to the Peloponnese, where beads of Baltic amber have been found in Mycenaean graves dating from the sixteenth century BC.

This was our route, based on an ancient path that has guided people for thousands of years. What would it be like now? How easy would it be to find small and interesting roads that roughly followed the historic trail? Would it be all right cycling? I had an idea that many country roads might still be cobbled. Would the people be nice? There were all kinds of questions that could not be answered, and the only detail we could fix with certainty was the date for departure: 2 June, 3.30 p.m., Scandinavian Seaways from Harwich to Hamburg.

1. POLAND

Once upon a time there was Europe.
Europe stretched from the Atlantic to the
Urals. It included Budapest, Prague and
Petersburg as well as Paris and Madrid.
No account of European culture could
ignore the voices of Kant from Königsberg,
or Tolstoy from Yasnaya Polyana. The
word 'revolution' was introduced to
European discourse by Copernicus from
Toruń. Before the First World War an
Englishman or American of means and
spirit could personally discover the whole
of this heritage passing freely, without
passport, let or hindrance, from Barcelona
to Kraków, or from Naples to Aberdeen.

Timothy Garton Ash,
The Polish Revolution, 1991

THE ROAD TO HEL

It was a very wobbly start indeed. In spite of last-minute trimming of our baggage, the 12 kilograms on the back of the bicycle weighed heavy on my sense of balance. Every time I set off, my bike leaned worryingly to the right, and I had to strain hard to cycle in a straight line while traffic thundered past on Kingsland High Road. The handlebars wobbled out of control at the slightest slip of my hands or attention, and I willed the traffic lights to stay green so I could avoid another inept start.

Drivers and pedestrians stared with incredulity at our laden bikes and by the time we reached Liverpool Street Station I was already hot with effort and nerves. How to indicate or change gears when you can't take your hands off the handlebars? I had hardly got used to doing it without any baggage, but now – I simply had to stay in the same gear, which meant I came to a standstill at the slightest incline.

My brand-new touring bike had no less than twenty-one gears, to be found by pushing two separate levers somewhere between my legs. How were you supposed to know what combination of large front chainwheel (choice of three) and rear sprocket (choice of seven) was best? To complicate matters even further the gear levers each went in opposite directions for taking their set of gears up or down, and I still could not remember which one did what in what direction.

Two short excursions had certainly not been enough to practise these things, not to mention get used to the strange drop handlebars that made you feel like your face was much too close to the road. I had to twist my neck just to see where I was going.

'You'll get used to it,' Benoît said, which seemed impossible at this stage and I wished I could have stuck to my original idea of buying a plain old bike in Poland. If it was good enough for the locals why not for us too? It was typically male, I thought, to insist on some high-tech model with competitive speed options. Of course I would shortly learn that our fancy machines were truly essential, but on that first day it seemed like I would never get the hang of it.

At Harwich docks there was a mini flyover to negotiate and, sure enough, I had to get off and push, holding up the traffic of impatient cars unable to pass my lurching bulk. Soon I would be in control of all this! But in the meantime I hid behind my dark sun-glasses and pretended I was pushing the bike on purpose.

Originally I wanted to take a cargo ship from Tilbury docks to the Polish port of Gdynia. However, much to the relief of Benoît, who fears the sea, the ship's handful of cabins had already been reserved. This was our next best option: to take a passenger boat from Harwich to Hamburg, which would take only twenty-two hours instead of five days, and then catch a train to the Polish border.

It was important to me to travel this way, overland and not by plane. I wanted to feel I was still in Europe, still travelling in the same part of the world that is now supposed to be all one. If this is so, we should be able to get to Poland with ease, not fly in as if it were the other side of the world. At least in our minds it would help to give us a sense of being close to accustomed territory.

We docked at Hamburg's St Pauli/Landungsbrücken shortly after midday and soon we were pedalling along the banks of the river Elbe, circling the outline of the ancient city, past fragrant warehouses packed with coffee, tea and oriental carpets. Giant hooks swung packages from beams jutting out of wood and redbrick gables, while miniature men waited to receive them in high-up lofts. We were on our way! All muscles straining to stay moving upright while my imagination raced ahead into the Polish distance.

Arrived at the *Hauptbahnhof*, we dodged beggars and drug addicts to reach the ticket hall, but not before I tripped on a pedal and crashed to the ground with a girlish yelp. If cycling a loaded bike is hard, pushing it is even worse, but I laughed sweatily and hoped no one could tell how embarrassed I was. There was no time to dwell anyway, because we quickly found ourselves rushing around in a frenzy of money-changing and ticket-buying. The train was leaving in twenty minutes.

'Why didn't you change some money on the boat?' we asked each other.

It was a strange feeling travelling on this train. I had taken the exact same route into the German Democratic Republic just four years earlier. Then the train had crossed the border through a frightening corridor of barbed wire and watch-towers. Uniformed men had got on to the train – about five for every wagon – and the passengers of each compartment were asked in turn to come out and stand in the corridor while their luggage was examined.

'Do you have anything to declare?' the customs man had asked, and I had shaken my face in silence, the illegal currency in my underpants warm against my skin. The official exchange rate was one East German mark to one West German mark, and I had changed at six to one in a Hamburg bank.

I spent two weeks in the former GDR, and discovered that the people were much friendlier than their watchdogs. Yet when it came time to leave, my new friends and I had sadly agreed we would probably never see each other again unless I returned. They would not be allowed out of their country until they were old and the State no longer cared if they tried to leave or not, and even then they would still need a relative in West Germany to apply for permission to travel there. We spoke in the privacy of their homes, closed off from treacherous ears.

That was how it was, and any idea that it could ever be different was simply fantasy. Yet a year and a half later the impossible had happened and, like millions of others, I had gone to Berlin to savour history first hand. One day I followed the breached Wall behind the *Reichstag*, where there was a stark reminder of the recent past: white crosses attached to a wire fence commemorated every person known to have died in at-tempted border crossings. One had been left blank except for the date, to indicate that the body was never identified, and someone's black felt pen had freshly added the name, the hand of a grieving relative perhaps, free for the first time publicly to mourn this person's death. The most recent cross was for a young man in his twenties, killed in February 1989. If only he could have waited nine months – he could have crossed without risking his life. But how could anyone have known?

The return journey, back in 1988, had been even more frightening than the arrival, with paranoid thoughts that they would not let me out or that they would confiscate my notes and papers. Instead, armed soldiers had searched for stowaways inside the train, while others banged metal bars underneath the carriages and sent sniffer dogs along the tracks. That was the reality then, yet now we rumbled comfortably through welcoming green countryside and, except for a fleeting glimpse of an abandoned platform, the old border had become invisible. My old acquaintances too have disappeared. The chaos of upheaval since the Wall came down has swept them away, and recent letters have gone unanswered.

'Oh, you are going to Poland?' Two elderly ladies nodded as I answered their enquiry.

Between themselves they spoke *plattdeutsch*, an almost unintelligible dialect that sounds more Dutch than German. Occasionally I understood some words, enough to know that they were gossiping about their village.

'Yes, and I went to him and I said, that sand is from my land you know, and I expect to be paid for it. Some people just have no manners. I mean, he thinks he can build himself a new house with God knows what money he got from somewhere, and then he doesn't even have the courtesy to ask. Well, I didn't let him get away with it.'

'No, of course you shouldn't,' her friend agreed.

'I'm a widow, after all, with no prospects for making new money now.'

The indignant one turned to me during a lull in their conversation.

'I went to Poland once, on a day trip across the border. You must be careful, especially of your money, because Polish people are very dishonest.'

'Why do you say that?'

'I took a bus to a village by the sea once, and when I got the return bus my ticket cost less than it did before. I had my money ready to give the driver, but he said it was too much. The other driver overcharged me,' she told me with a damning nod, 'and I have never been back to Poland. My children go sometimes, but not me.'

Happily, our first day in Poland was a much better experience.

We cycled across the border and into Swinoujście (pronounced Shwinn-o-oosh-chye) the next morning. The town was a rather drab combination of working port and tourist resort. However, since it was our first day, we decided to stay the night here to acclimatise a little and change some money. We intended to spend the time it would take to reach Gdańsk getting fit, and it suited us well to spend an afternoon plotting easy stages along the coast.

Looking around for the tourist information I approached a man on the street for directions. He spoke neither German nor English, but we managed to communicate somehow and, before we knew it, we had followed him to the local tourist office, where he proceeded to tell an astounded member of staff that we could stay with him. All I could understand was the word 'gratis' coming from him, while the lady was firmly shaking her head. She told me that if we wished to stay with this man, we should pay him 80,000 zlotys, which was about US$3 each and seemed reasonable to us.

Juliusz, as our host was called, turned out to be a ship's cook on a tanker that travelled the world from New York to Karachi. What luck! A place to stay and our host a cook. Soon we were eating our first Polish *kiełbasa* (sausage) with bread and admiring Juliusz's photos of his ship and all the exotic places he had seen without ever having spoken to anyone except his Polish crew mates.

His house was a fine three-storey building set in a dusty clearing among utilitarian high-rises. His family had spent five years clubbing together to build it, and there were no less than three bathrooms, one on every floor. Not only that, but through his travels to all the world's duty-free shops, he had amassed a hoard of electrical goods, from the latest large-screen television to a cordless telephone. It was very impressive and could have matched the gadgets in any Western European household. The only difference was the signed picture of the Pope over the sitting-room fireplace, and the tiny old Polski Fiat parked in the spare room.

Outside, his prize possession was locked in the garage along with our bikes: a bright-red VW Golf diesel. Considering the average Polish wage in 1992 was US$200 per month, he must have saved very hard for that car. Perhaps it was second-hand, but it looked sparkling new to us.

He took us out for a spin, and we toured the sights in ten minutes. The most notable buildings in town were the old Soviet base and military hospital that made up an entire block, framed in leafy streets once home to the nineteenth-century bourgeoisie. Only 'Russkis' could be treated in the hospital, Juliusz told us. Local people had to make do with a dilapidated medical centre elsewhere, and it was obvious no one was going to mourn the Russian departure, which was bound to happen soon.

The windswept beach stretched far into the tideless distance, and we walked close to protective sand dunes, bushels of rough grass and knobbly spruce rustling in our ears. Behind the dunes an endless promenade drew a straight line where one trinket and ice-cream seller shouldered another. There were even amber stalls, and I could hardly resist buying a necklace there and then. The word for amber was *bursztyn*, a Polish version of the original German, *Bernstein*.

In the evening Juliusz's wife Zofia came home from work, and we had more animated conversations in English. She was a bouncy lady with a big smile and she soon confirmed what I thought I had understood at the tourist office: that we must stay for free.

'When I travelled to the United States people were so kind and generous to me. Now we can pay it back by being generous to you. I think one should always be generous to foreign guests,' she reassured us. Clearly hers was a lucky family. Both she and Juliusz worked for foreign companies and were unlikely to loose their jobs during their country's present economic struggle.

Reading the Western press I had imagined that people here barely had enough to eat, let alone had the latest video machine. It was an idea so strongly formed that it stuck with me throughout this journey. Yet the further south we travelled, the more absurd my worries became, and most of the food I had insisted on buying in England was never used, eventually given away in Serbia where they needed it least of all.

The pain in my thighs was only just subsiding, six hours after arriving in Kamień Pomorski, around 53 kilometres east of Swinoujście. The flat and windless stretches shaded by cooling forests of oak and beech were wonderful – as close to flying as you can get. But the occasional hills were agonising and the coastal wind was no help either. The last 12 kilometres were pure hell. More than once my leg muscles gave out and I collapsed by the roadside, a pathetic sight for Benoît, who kindly said nothing until later.

You are supposed to breathe only through your nose in conditions like this, so as to loose the least amount of body fluid. Trouble was, crushing the pedals up and down my mouth inevitably opened to let out gasps of effort and, to make things worse, my nose was blocked with hay fever. On the downhill my immediate problem was to change gears back to a tougher notch without loosing control of the bike at the same time. It was always a dangerous moment. I still had not mastered balancing the weight of the bicycle, and my fingers seemed just a little too short to reach the brake levers beyond my handlebars. I narrowly missed head-diving into the tarmac about three times on that first day.

The only part of the journey's routine that was becoming easier was the packing and loading of the bike. About six kilograms filled each pannier, while the front handlebar bag held my camera and papers, and fitting them on to their hooks was a reassuring ritual when I got it right. All you needed then was not to forget to fill your water-bottle, to put on the cycling gloves and sun-glasses, and you were ready to roll.

It was a nerve-racking stage these first few days, but it was also exhilarating. When I found myself cruising well I had time to notice the Baltic countryside, which was beautiful. Pine and conifer along the beaches gave way to deciduous forest further inland, while poplars or chestnut trees held country lanes in a dancing shade. The roadsides were sprinkled with tiny yellow flowers and edging the young wheat fields, blue cornflowers and carmine poppies swayed in the breeze.

Horse-drawn haymakers were a common sight, and picturesque red-brick farms offered fleeting glances of ramshackle yards. Usually the family home was at a right angle to the barn, with the stables and cow shed opposite creating a cosy square facing the road. Carts and farming tools littered these spaces, while above it all a huge stork's nest was often enthroned on the chimney stack. So gawky when they flew or landed, standing still on one leg they were utterly regal and mysterious. Closer to the ground, swallows darted around our bikes, and we both felt sure they were following us. They ducked and dived through the air just like dolphins chasing a boat.

From Kamień Pomorski we cycled a tough 70 kilometres to Kołobr-zeg, which means 'beside the coast', and again I huffed and puffed, and sweat made my sun-glasses slide down my nose with maddening fre-quency. Hills are one thing, but wind is quite another, and when you have the wind against you every pedal stroke is an effort, flat or hilly. Combine the two and you have the most demoralising conditions barring rain, and I swore into the wind throughout the day.

Meanwhile my hay fever was getting worse. My nose was almost constantly blocked but running, my eyes were swollen and my throat was itchy. At night, Benoît said, I sounded like a whistling train, and he refused to sleep in the same bed, retiring elsewhere armed with ear-plugs. My only consolation was a soft pillow. Neither of us could face camping yet and, since the hotels were cheap, we treated ourselves to hot showers and comfortable sleeping quarters.

I wrote in bed, propped up by pillows and legs glowing with Deep Heat to soothe my aching muscles. So far I knew three Polish words: *tak* for 'yes', *nie wiem* for 'I don't know', and *dziękuje* for 'thank you'. It was not much, but it was a start. At least we could point to places on our map when asking for directions and thank the person afterwards. Of course understanding their answer was quite another matter and had already led to great confusion.

Looking for a hotel in Kamień Pomorski, we had approached the postman as a likely advisor. He was a chubby man bursting out of his dark-blue uniform and a small cap perched above a jolly face. When I showed him my piece of paper he immediately launched into directions and jabbed the air or cupped his hands to indicate straight on or round a corner. The words *lewo* and *prawo* cropped up a lot, but I was a long time from knowing that meant 'left' and 'right'. It was impossible. I could not understand a single word. He tried again, speaking louder and slower while I smiled helplessly. In the end he just gave up, shrugged his shoulders and walked off. Stupid tourists!

The north-west of Poland used to be part of German Pomerania, while east of Gdańsk was part of East Prussia from the fifteenth century onwards. I had expected the old language to be understood. This was a mistake, however, because the German population was expelled after the Second World War and replaced by Polish citizens from eastern territories lost to Russia. Their descendants have never had occasion to learn German and not many of the former inhabitants ever returned. If anything, English is more useful, since that is the favoured language now taught in Polish schools. 'Ethnic cleansing' is by no means a new concept, and has caused misery in many countries.

The Oder–Neisse border between Germany and Poland is as artificial as the Berlin Wall. The last few centuries offer no basis for it and that will no doubt always be remembered in certain quarters. With recent territorial agreements ratified, it seems unlikely that the division will be overturned, but the young borders of Central and Eastern Europe are a potentially dangerous legacy that is clear for all to see.

Yugoslavia is only the most obvious example of how unstable this part of the world is. All the national borders in the region are as volatile as shifting earth plates, and huge quakes and eruptions could still occur at any time. From Poland to Greece people are looking over their shoulders with unease, and this fear and ancient hatreds are creating a tension we were to sense increasingly the further south we travelled.

Our good feelings from the first day in Poland were soon to be severely dampened. We decided to take a train to the bay of Gdańsk to speed up arrival at what we considered the proper starting point for the amber trail. We knew it might be a bit of a palaver travelling with the bikes, but we never imagined it would be *that* tough.

The trouble began on the platform. Having found out which *peron* (platform) the train was leaving from, we were unable to discover where to position ourselves for the baggage wagon. Should we wait at either end or in the middle? We tried to gesticulate our question to other passengers, but they just stared at us dumbly or shrugged their shoulders. It seemed obvious enough to us what we were asking for, but no one cared to understand – or so it seemed.

The train arrived and there was a rush for seats. There was no baggage compartment. Instead, we had to strip the bikes, fling a total of seven pieces of luggage past the train door, and then lift the bikes up three metal steps and into the corridor between two wagons. The trains were the old kind, where the doors are high above the ground. All this had to be done in less than three minutes, and by the time the whistle blew we fell exhausted into our seats. Luckily the train was not very full and having stowed the bags away, we hoped people would not mind skirting around our bicycles near the door.

We sat in a compartment with six others, who stared at us but never smiled. I tried to smile and make eye contact, but found only expressionless eyes gazing back in return. It was unnerving being looked at like that. There was no connection between us, not even the most basic kind of human recognition. Perhaps we were unlucky, but it made me feel every bit the stranger in a foreign land. Even when we did manage to communicate people seemed incapable of taking the initiative. In

Kołobrzeg we had asked a woman for a certain hotel, and she directed us to it, just two blocks further. Only when we got there it was an empty building site, something she must have known but neglected to tell us.

The train shortly arrived at a large station where the platform teemed with people waiting to climb aboard. Now the trouble really began, for the bikes were blocking a door to the second-class compartments. I tried to gesture that perhaps they should better use another door, like the one immediately adjacent. But no. The crowd must use this door and a man forced it open, causing our front wheels to jerk upwards with the flipping of the floor panel connected to the opening door. A riptide of people pushed up the steps and into the corridor, straight away entangled by pieces of jutting bicycle and me trying to straighten them out to move away. It was an instant blockage. Could they not see that if they did not give me time to move it was impossible to ease a passage? The crowd moved in like a suffocating wave, forcing their way past me, muttering abuse and regularly giving me a vicious shove for good measure. A bulging lady nudged me with her fleshy body and I snapped at her to wait just a moment, pronouncing the word in a panic-stricken combination of German and Spanish.

I cried for Benoît's help, but there was too much noise for him to hear me. At last some passengers decided to use the other door or move down the platform, and the whistle blew the final call. Nerves and body badly shaken, I returned to my seat. What was wrong with these people? Clearly we were causing an obstruction, but why this uncompromising attitude? It was a profoundly stressful experience that left me dumbly staring out of the window.

A new passenger lit up a cigarette in the already stifling compartment. I opened the window a little for some fresh air, but no sooner had I sat down than the young man got up and closed it again. No words were spoken, and the others just gazed on as if nothing had happened. It was baffling and alienating and my spirits sank. I went out to check on the bikes and stepped on the man's foot on the way out. Two can play at this game I festered to myself. Later the man confused me even further by offering me a cigarette.

Perhaps we were simply too strange and ridiculous for these country people and, rather like the proverbial village idiot, the object of chicanery, abuse and good will all at once. Or perhaps, as obvious members of the privileged West (obvious because of our fancy bikes and foreign language), we were the easy target for the deep anger and resentment many Poles are feeling because of their country's failure to offer them a better life – it was a depressing aspect of our journey that we came up against repeatedly and not just in Poland. There was an invisible barrier between us that had nothing to do with language or prejudice, but rather with local conditions of deprivation and shattered hopes.

We had to change trains twice more, and each time our adrenalin raced against the clock as we loaded or unloaded, not to mention moved to another platform. Hel was our destination – a fitting name for the way we felt that day. In fact the place is a charming peninsula that hovers over the bay of Gdańsk like an old-fashioned car indicator. Never more than a hundred metres wide, a ridge of wind-bent spruce and conifers separate beaches of the finest white sand, and wild rosehip bushes line sandy paths among the dunes. A branch line reaches all the way to the very tip, but we got off about halfway down, in a village called Jastarnia.

It was early evening by now, and the village had already rolled up the pavements and the inhabitants gone home. Only a small snack bar was open, tucked away by the railway track, and we rode there eagerly, hoping for some food. At last we were out of those awful trains and sitting peacefully in the sunshine. Both of us agreed that spending a day travelling by train had been much tougher than cycling 70 kilometres, and we cheered ourselves up by eating our first Baltic flounder. We were served two small fish each, and they seemed almost too pretty to eat, with their flat bodies and dorsal fins matching the curve of our plates.

We found a campsite by the beach and set up the tent on a soft bed of pine needles. It was easy and we wondered why we had been so reticent to camp before. To be honest, it had not just been exhaustion that sent us to hotels. We were simply nervous about the practicalities of putting the tent up and I was secretly worried that if Benoît really hated it, he might mutiny straight away.

Here on the beach, however, watching swans sedately gliding by on the smooth waters, we both felt reassured. Crabs came out of their underground homes near our feet, while bobbing worm catchers stalked the wet sand. On the horizon we imagined being able to see the lights of Gdańsk across the bay. The great port was only 20 kilometres by sea and tomorrow we would be there. The anxiety of the day's events gradually faded with the setting sun, and we slept very well, in spite of my rasping breath.

In the morning I crossed the peninsula to see the maritime side. A swathe of sand rose gently from the foaming waves, and a bright seaside light cast the scene in vivid contrast. Sodden driftwood rose black-brown from the breathing sand and a million shell fragments crunched under my feet. The Hel beaches are some of the most popular recreational grounds on the Polish coast, yet they were already renowned almost two thousand years ago – not for their beauty, but for the amber that was thrown up by autumn seas until just a few centuries ago, when overexploitation exhausted supplies.

The Bronze Age people of the Baltic bartered amber for weapons and tools or exchanged it for precious ornaments from distant parts, such as glass beads from Syria that came to them via cultures living on the Danubian plain. Not until the Romans did amber become an item of trade in itself. Then it was brought to their northerly border posts by the 'barbarian' tribes from beyond their empire and merchants paid for it with gold coins. This must have seemed very strange to the northern cultures at the time, because theirs was still a code of 'finders keepers'. Only much later, in the early Middle Ages, did amber gathering become controlled by the ruling powers of society, and it was the Teutonic Knights (1225–1525) who first established a state monopoly on amber exploitation and trade.

Medieval books show engravings of amber gatherers, armed with nets on the end of poles (*Käscher*), prospecting in the water. For amber is a porous mass, which usually contains pockets of gas, so it can be caught swimming in the waves, just like fish. (Its specific gravity is generally 1.08, which means it can float in sea water, but not fresh water). In fact, my favourite image for amber touches on this unique feature, and was conjured up by the poet, Matthew Arnold, who likened waves to 'a ceiling of amber' whirling on to 'a pavement of pearl' (from *The Forsaken Merman*).

Most of the amber catch would have been for the craftsmen in Gdańsk, but there were many uses for amber other than ornamentation: burning it produced a fragrant incense recalling the pine forests it once came from, while infusions made from it were used for home remedies. Some believed, even in this century, that amber wards off infertility, and in the

Polish town of Ostrołeka daughters were traditionally given amber necklaces on their wedding day.

Since amber has always been most likely to appear after winter storms, in November and December, gathering during medieval times was a dangerous business. The men had to spend many hours standing on the edge of rough seas, all roped together like mountaineers, and the only protective clothing they had were chest-high suits of leather trousers, and jackets insulated with wool. Often the wet leather froze to their bodies and women kept constant fires burning on the beaches, so the men could thaw out before filling their amber into sacks and walking home.

There were other ways of gathering amber, but they depended on calm seas. For example, a method called *Bernstein stecken* (hooking) involved using small boats near the shore, from which men tried to dislodge chunks of amber trapped under large boulders with 10–30-foot poles topped by iron semi-circular hooks. Sometimes they would even dive underwater, but that must have been a last resort. Later, in the seventeenth century, these hazardous methods were abandoned for dredging the sea-bed and, in 1862, the first steam-powered dredgers were used on the Samland peninsula, on the eastern side of the bay of Gdańsk.

Of course, the most productive method of amber gathering was – and still is – mining, which was first done on a large scale in the seventeenth century. Huge pits were dug along the coast, where men and women shovelled in permanently cold and wet conditions that must have been just as unhealthy as standing in waves.

With its natural warmth and mysterious origin there undoubtedly is something magical about amber, and I looked forward to seeing a lot more of it in Gdańsk, where amber craftsmen still follow their trade, just as they have done for hundreds of years. I hurried back to my waiting companion and we set off with brisk morning energy. The wind was in our backs for once, and we cruised with easy speed between the railway line and the open beach.

ON THE AMBER TRAIL

Arrived in Gdańsk we were soon approached by an old woman speaking German. It was good to be spoken to in a language I could understand.

'*Wollen Sie ein Zimmer?*' (Do you need a room?), she asked, and we were willing customers. It was a relief not to have to search any further, and the chance to stay with a local family was always preferable.

Other ladies hovered around us like benevolent crows, but we had already been collared with determined friendliness. Professional eyes appraised our worth from a distance as we haggled over a price, and it was not long before we agreed on 500,000 zlotys for three nights. At about US$36 it was double what we had been paying so far, but we were in one of the country's most famous cities and for that it was excellent value. There are no cities in Western Europe where you could get a double room for US$12.

On the way to her house the woman tried to up the price. Her eagerness to secure our custom had outpaced her maths. Walking slowly, her face wrinkled with second thoughts, she tried for an extra 100,000 zlotys. It was hard not to relent with guilty feelings of wealth, but I was vindicated the next day when I discovered that our agreed fee was equal to one week's rent on a council flat. She had done well out of us and her married daughter did not mind giving us the children's room.

Our new home was not far from the centre, in a nineteenth-century block of flats with a creaky wooden stairwell and pigeons warbling in the enclosed courtyard. A musky smell of polish and coal greeted us at the entrance. Below street level a dark warren of cellar partitions was filled with ancient bric-à-brac where we left the bikes, and then it was a slow climb of nearly a hundred steps to the fourth floor.

Our window looked on to the spacious courtyard where a huge tree made up the centrepiece. There was a metal bar for beating carpets, perfect for swinging upside-down, and the cries of playing children mixed with domestic sounds from their homes above.

The conniving continued even in the flat. I asked if there was a shower, to which she replied: 'Yes, certainly we have a shower, and hot water costs so much money ...'

In our room she pointed to one of the children's beds: 'You can sleep in this bed, can't you?'

'But it's a single,' Benoît protested.

'Yes, but you know, washing powder is so expensive and this way I only have to wash one set of sheets ...'

But she relented quickly. She was basically a good woman, and when we returned in the evening to wash our clothes with our own washing powder, she did not object, and even helped us put them out to dry on her balcony. She had a well-worn motherliness about her that softened the edges of her business instinct.

Her name was Gertrude, born in Germany she told me – here in *Danzig*, before the war. But her entire family had been expelled, like hundreds of thousands of other Germans, who used to make up over 95 per cent of this town's population. Only she had returned. Her German was very rusty by now, but she could still manage it well enough. Well enough to entice German-speaking visitors to stay with her before they reached the official accommodation office.

If at our arrival in Poland we had been lucky, we were equally unlucky on our first day in Gdańsk. We walked into the city in the evening, looking for a meal and somewhere to change money and, by the time we reached the glamorous centre, half a dozen money-changers had approached us on the street.

'Don't change money on the street,' everyone had warned us, and I cautiously walked on. But Benoît, ever the bloodhound for special offers, went back to check the rate of one particular man. We had done it so many times in Latin America, why should it be any different here? The rate was good – a bit too good, I thought – but the dealing had already begun and we turned down a side alley.

The man counted 700,000 zlotys on to his palm and I checked they were 100,000 notes and not the similar 1,000 notes. Everything seemed fine, though he appeared tense and fingered Benoît's US$50 note while still holding on to his money.

'Is it a good fifty?' he asked suspiciously.

'Sure it is. Is your money as good?' we joked.

'Why don't you check it in a shop to see it's real?' he replied.

'No, no. That's all right. We're sure,' we said without any basis at all. The deal was clinched and then …

'Oh, quick, someone is coming!' and there was.

Automatically we exchanged the cash quickly and left. It crossed my mind that changing money on the street might be illegal.

'So you changed the money all right?' I asked, walking ahead.

'It was easy,' I heard, and next: 'Oh shit. He got me.'

He ran back to an empty street and I found him pacing around in a rage. The man had switched the money at the last moment, and instead of 700,000 zlotys, we had only 7,000, worth about fifty US cents at the time.

It was a good lesson, but it was a depressing one that made us like Poland less that evening, especially since we had still not quite recovered from the abrasive train experience two days earlier. Of course it was Benoît's own fault, but that made it no easier to accept. I tried to cheer him up by saying it was fate: the lost money was just what he would have spent if we had taken a hotel room.

Things looked better the next day. We found a small bakery near Gertrude's selling delicious fresh doughnuts, a cheap coffee bar in town and a friendly crowd on the streets of Gdańsk.

The city has a certain flair about it and people walk with confidant strides. Perhaps recent history, since the birth of *Solidarność* in 1980, has taught its citizens self-assurance. Yet the movement has split and there must be less and less work in the shipyards. Perhaps the economic boost tourism has brought here, as well as the regular exposure to foreigners, has made them less wary and more receptive. At any rate, there was a good atmosphere. Along the waterfront there were lively stands for beer and chips, and the market was full of every kind of fruit and vegetable you could wish for, not to mention a mouthwatering selection of home-made sausages and all kinds of bread and pastries. I laughed to think of the packet soups in my pannier.

In the old quarter, baroque gables recall other Hanseatic cities, while the occasional canal and tall narrow houses remind of Amsterdam. Its heart is almost entirely post–Second World War restoration, but you can hardly tell. Surrounding the city, ugly concrete housing estates sit like giant breeze blocks on the flat countryside. But if you stay in the centre, the narrow cobblestone streets, the Gothic redbrick churches and the elegant façades of traditional burgher's homes create a pleasant mixture of grace and history.

A particularly fine street is Mariachi, where one sparkling jewellery shop shoulders another. Silver is the predominant setting for amber it seems, and there were pieces of all shapes and sizes made into anything from brooches and necklaces, to ear-rings and bracelets. The reigning style was a rather florid art nouveau, all curls and expansive bows that I did not like much.

I searched for a shop name that might indicate a German speaker, and instead found a proprietor who spoke excellent English. His name was Mr Shablovsky[1] and his family had been in the amber business for several decades

'So where does the amber come from that you use in your shop?'

'Oh, it's all Russian.'

'That's strange, isn't it? I would have thought you'd use Polish amber, in Gdańsk of all places.'

'No, no. That's much too expensive. We buy our amber from thieves,' he said with an enigmatic twinkle.

'How's that?'

'Well, they smuggle it from Russia, and we buy it. You see, Polish amber costs too much so we have to buy contraband to make our business worthwhile.

'The largest mine in the world is at Jantarny near Kaliningrad, not far from the Polish–Lithuanian border. *Janta* means amber in Russian and, but for the German background of this region, it should be called something similar in Polish. Along the Lithuanian Baltic, amber deposits are only eight metres under the ground, so mining for it is easy.

'In Poland, on the other hand, it is mostly 200 metres underground, which makes it too expensive to mine. Occasionally Polish amber is still used. Such as ten years ago, when they dug a new port at Pólnocny and

[1] Not his real name.

found large deposits by chance. You can even still find it on the beaches. But there are many more people looking than pieces to be found.'

Mr Shablovsky was very free with his information and it was not long before he was telling us a bit about himself. In his youth he had been conscripted into the Polish navy, aged nine, only to be taken off by the Russians, who set him to work in the barren salt mines past the Ural mountains.

'Yes, I was in Siberia,' he nodded, 'it was two years before I could leave, when I was fourteen. Of course it wasn't really Siberia. But for us Poles all of Russia is Siberia.'

It had taken him many years to make his way home, first finding himself taken back by the Polish navy, who sent him to Iran and then to Egypt. It was a long time before he settled in Gdańsk and even then he was not in his true home. His family came from a part of Poland now belonging to Russia and there was no returning there.

Told on a sunny day in 1992, his life story sounded rather exotic to young travellers like us, and his smiling face showed no self-pity or signs of the hardship and sorrow he must have experienced. Deportation and displacement were the fate of many of his generation, but he seemed to be at peace with that – happy to enjoy his successful business in old age and send his granddaughter to America to learn English.

Gdańsk turned out to be a fruitful place for meeting interesting people. Another day I met Piotr in the café we had found on our first morning. He was a sports yachtsman who had raced for Poland in international competitions, but was now reduced to earning a living as a builder. The State no longer subsidises international sporting events such as sailing, and without sponsorship from Polish businesses there are no crews or boats to represent the country any more.

'The new system has brought no improvements. Not one! he grumbled. What is the point of being in Europe if we only get paid 20 per cent of Western European salaries? I have to work in East Germany so I can earn a decent wage. Here in Poland it is impossible. There is no work, and when there is they pay you almost nothing.' Yellow fingers held a thin cigarette to his lips.

'So you think the old system was better? You want it back?'

'No, no. Of course not. Now we have democratic freedom. Only in

Poland democracy is a political cabaret. Do you know we have over two hundred parties? Who are we supposed to vote for?'

'What about Lech Wałęsa?'

'How can a simple electrician rule a country? He was a good leader of workers in eighty-one, courageous and single-minded. But he is no politician. And anyway, we don't need politicians, we need economists.'

'So with economic investment there is still hope though, isn't there?'

'No. There is no hope. Poland missed its chance and now the West is not interested. Our market is too small for them and so we are lost. The West simply skips Poland to invest in the huge potential of the former Soviet Union. We have nothing because we have nothing they want.'

In fact, Poland's grain harvest is second only to France, while its potato crop is as large as all of Europe's put together. Trouble is, the European Community, made up of Western European countries with subsidised farming, is not about to let cheap farming produce from Eastern Europe flood their market. The Iron Curtain has been lifted but the Economic Barrier has replaced it.

'So there is really no hope?'

'Poland is a great big mess and the people are very angry. I think the future could easily be civil war.'

'But that's terrible,' I said rather uselessly.

'Yes, it is terrible.'

'But don't you think with patience ...'

'No! No more. All my life under communism I was told "Be quiet, be patient." There is NO MORE patience.'

There are plenty of people who feel like Piotr and democratic freedom has turned out to be a hall of mirrors. Appearances constantly deceive: they are free to travel, but they have no money, and even money is not enough. Many countries are still operating (or freshly instituting) restrictive visa requirements against Eastern Europeans, fearful of a huge immigrant problem. The meanness is bad enough, but the arrogance of it is worse. A common remark I encountered was: 'I don't want to live in a foreign country, away from my home, family and friends. I just want to see what it's like. Like you coming here.' No wonder we met with occasional hostility.

The disillusion can be found at many levels of society. As someone in Hungary was to point out to me: before the fall of communism it was much easier to gain shelter abroad; while artists and intellectuals enjoyed a willing audience in the West. It was chic to support banned or imprisoned writers, but now they are 'free' their Western fans have quickly forgotten them and the recession has meant they can get published neither in their own country nor abroad.

Meeting Piotr was a sobering experience and made me realise that the sullenness we had encountered in the countryside was not an unpleasant cultural characteristic, but the symptom of a sick spirit. There is a sense of grave disappointment. Unemployment (officially 12 per cent in 1992) and soaring prices are at the forefront of many people's minds, and it is tempting for some to put a rosy haze on the former system, where everyone knew what to expect. The shops may not have had much, but at least you could always get what you needed eventually. The State took care of you. And now? The shops are full of things few can afford and the authorities appear to be wasting time and money on frivolous changes like renaming the streets with communist heroes or anniversaries. Capitalism is not like it was on the television.

Someone who saw it slightly differently was Darek, an unemployed oceanographer fresh out of university. We met him in a student bar, where he had approached us, eager to speak English and make Western contacts. He had spent a year in the United States and seen the bastion of capitalism for himself and not liked it much.

'All that choice. It's depressing,' he said, and I knew just what he meant. I have often wished someone else could be responsible for my choices. On the other hand, the alternative has been proved even more depressing.

Darek did not care who ran the country or what system was used, as long as he could get a job in his chosen profession and travel abroad at least once a year. He was selfish but honest. Conveniently he was also a fatalist, so his unemployment and poor prospects for doing any of the things he wished to do did not overly depress him yet. He would bide his time, and as long as he had some money to drink with his friends, he did not care what the world got up to. Alcohol, at least, was still extremely cheap.

He was not interested in politics and in that he was more representative of young people's attitude than the much described student and worker activists. From Poland southwards we met plenty of young people with opinions but, like Darek, they wanted to mind their own business, get on with their own lives and forget the rest. Perhaps that too is disaffection, but mass participation in the political process is a rare event anywhere and only exceptional circumstances bring people out. The euphoria of 1980 in Poland and of 1989 for the rest of Eastern Europe has been smothered. Already it seems hard to imagine that one ever felt it.

We left our host and the 'bright lights' of Gdańsk to head south. Our first destination was Malbork, formerly known as Marienburg, and one of the greatest of all the Teutonic castles built along a 180-kilometre stretch of the river Vistula, from the coast to Toruń.

The Teutonic Knights were a German order of military monks that evolved after the Crusades, with no connection to Poland until Prince Conrad the Mazovian made the mistake of inviting them to establish themselves at Chełmno in 1226. The Prince thought he could use the Order to stave off attacks from neighbouring forces, such as the Lithuanians and Prussians. Instead the Knights quickly established their own power base on Polish territory, cuckoo rulers in someone else's nest, and built the impressive fortresses to affirm their status and control the lucrative grain trade carried on the river.

They excelled not only in battle but also in business, and the amber trade came under their monopoly, ensuring them great profits. Exploitation and crafting were strictly controlled, and it is said that once a forest of gallows cast their shadow along the coast. Death by hanging was the punishment for unlawful amber gathering or digging.

In fact, hanging of unauthorised amber gatherers continued right up until the eighteenth century, when beach inspectors regularly patrolled the Baltic coast. In later times, punishments were gauged by the amount stolen, and ranged from beating with rods, imprisonment, banishment, compulsory labour, to death. It is an indication of just how valuable amber was, that each adult had to make an official oath every three years not to steal amber, and to denounce anyone who did – a law that was only abolished in 1811.

To stop illicit working of this precious substance no workshops were permitted inside the Knights' territory. Instead, distant craftsmen, as far away as Bruges, were sent the raw material, and not until the fifteenth century, when the Teutonic Knights were finally defeated, were workshops legalised on the Polish Baltic, most importantly in Gdańsk.

35

It was the combined military might of the Poles and Lithuanians that eventually crushed the Knights' power at the Battle of Grünwald, in 1410. But they managed to remain in the region for another fifty-six years by retreating to Malbork Castle, where they stayed until the Treaty of Toruń forced them to leave and make a brief and final headquarters in Kaliningrad (Königsberg) before the Order was dissolved. (The militaristic East Prussian state was their heir, a powerful legacy right up until this century.) Malbork Castle suitably has the largest collection of amber in the world, and it was this that I especially wanted to see.

The fortifications throne high above the river, immense redbrick walls rising up to rounded towers and pointy turrets. Vertical slits along custodial walkways present guarded openings to the outside world, and the only entrance is via a series of iron-grilled archways, where all but friends would have been certain of a dousing of boiling oil and a hail of lances. We arrived close to sunset, and the whole mountainous construction glowed in a magnificent rusty outline.

The cobbled inner plaza resounded to the squabbles of excited schoolchildren and prancing crows, and we mingled among them to squeeze into ancient dungeons, courtly reception rooms and sooty kitchens where great cauldrons used to boil. The castle is a maze of corridors and courtyards, all fitting together in a grand scheme to show the visitor how mighty its masters once were.

At last we reached the amber collection, blinds drawn to protect it from destructive sunlight and exhibits enclosed in thick glass casings to keep out the oxidising air. (Sadly, once exposed, amber eventually becomes so brittle that it falls to dust the moment it is touched.) Only the cases stood lit up in the twilight, their glow creating an almost festive atmosphere. The first exhibit was a large piece of rough amber, the size of a bear's head. Its rough and jagged edges were a caramel opaque and gave no hint of the beauty it contained.

It is extraordinary what amber can be made into: anything from engraved discs, cups and bowls, beads and hairpins, to intricately carved crucifixes, jewellery boxes and candlesticks; even commodes and mirror frames. The versatility of this mineral is equal to wood, except that the colouring is far more varied and the material much more fragile. I had always imagined amber as honey and gold coloured. Yet here there were pieces that ranged from crystal transparency to all shades of yellow, toffee and brown, as well as ivory white. In fact, there are also occurrences of green, blue, red and black amber, though these are very rare indeed.

The earliest examples of worked amber come from prehistoric times: amulets and beads, as well as small animal and human figurines used for pagan worship. But the most impressive exhibits date from the sixteenth and seventeenth centuries, when secular objects such as furniture and engraved portrait medallions started to be made for the Baltic nobles. The delicacy of the carving is truly remarkable, with whole groups of figures rising out of a single piece, completely belying the fragility of the material. Chess sets made with shades of brown and ivory amber were also beautiful.

Larger pieces, such as caskets, cabinets and writing desks, were made by cutting plates of amber and gluing them to a wooden base, often with gold foil in between to highlight engravings on the surface. These too were shown here, easily outshining the few twentieth-century exhibits, which were bulbous pieces of jewellery and decorative cups. The taste among modern artists seems to be to encrust metal and silver with shapeless lumps that cling to smooth surfaces like horrible growths.

The most famous piece of amber craftsmanship disappeared in mysterious circumstances. King Frederick I of Prussia commissioned an amber chamber shortly after his coronation in 1701, intended as a unique work of art, the like of which no other monarch had ever enjoyed. It took ten years to make and was the pride and joy of his Berlin castle. Every surface of the room was covered with a mosaic of carved amber panels, all in glorious hues of golden brown, creating a splendour reminiscent of marble, yet so much warmer.

For unclear reasons, however, the Russian Tsar, Peter I, ended up in possession of the room, which was transported panel for panel to his summer residence at Tsarskoe Selo. There it stayed until the Second World War, 'a perfect miracle' according to one visitor, who marvelled at the elegant panels depicting allegories of the five senses.

When the Germans were approaching during the Second World War, the panels were dismantled and stowed away. Unfortunately, however, they were not concealed well enough, and the Nazis stole them and had them mounted in the castle at Königsberg.

Did Allied bombs destroy them there or were they dismounted and hidden away once more? Nobody knows. All that is certain is that the single known example of an amber interior was lost. Apparently Russian artists are trying to recreate the panels, but in the absence of detailed design records the result seems doubtful.

From Malbork we cycled south, following the Vistula through the lower domain of the Teutonic Knights. The countryside remained mercifully flat and we spent hours gliding under the green arcades of tree-lined byways. Some of these were cobbled, just as I had feared, and the bones in our necks and buttocks rattled painfully, even cycling slowly.

Lines of poplars signalled streams and rivers in the distance, and every now and then barking dogs and chattering geese announced a farm. Inland, traditional farmhouses were often made entirely of wood, with a neat kitchen garden planted between the house and the road. Sometimes we would see a gang of women hoeing among the endless rows of potatoes or cabbages, while men sat postilion behind horse-drawn ploughs, a whip trailing behind them like a loose fishing line. Now and then we even saw a man pushing a small plough himself, a reminder that these fields were not in a West European countryside.

There were other signs in the towns: every evening inhabitants came out of their homes to gather at certain corners. Each person carried some kind of bottle or container and a farmer would be parked there, dispensing fresh milk from a great vat. It reminded me of childhood years when it was my job to fetch milk from the neighbouring farmer. We had a special one-litre can and if you swung your arm like a windmill the milk stayed in, even upside-down. Kids here did just the same.

By now we had established a comfortable rhythm that allowed us to make up to 70 kilometres per day, which was no great distance, and Benoît could have cycled much faster and further than I. But speed was not the object, and he almost always accepted the pace I set, rarely making me feel inadequate by cycling on ahead. Some days he would try to imperceptibly up the tempo, but I am sorry to say he soon reached my limit. I always suggested that he should take off for a while, but he rarely did and we took it in turns to cycle one behind the other.

Often we fell into a silent trance, in a kind of mindless concentration on the physical motion of bike and body, until it was inevitably me who called for a break. My leg muscles were still painful, but the exhilaration of feeling more in control of the bike was good compensation. I was able to swing and dodge a bit, in spite of the weight, and to speed downhill without using the brakes. I could even take my hand off the handlebars long enough to drink from my water-bottle – but only going slow, I admit. In the evenings we laughed at each other's legs, which looked very silly by now. Not because of amazing muscle build, but because, undressed, we looked as if we were wearing brown stockings. Our cycling pants cut a distinct line above the knee where suntanned skin gave way to pasty white.

Beyond Malbork we passed through three more fortified towns, the first of which was Grudziądz. The town was a pleasant surprise. Unlike almost every other we had seen so far, it seemed to have some colour to it, not the uniform drabness of post-communism. Many walls were freshly painted in traditional pastel colours, and shop windows were stocked with goods galore. There were even fancy clothes for sale and creative window displays. So often shop windows still showed the dead face of the old system, tins stacked in boring rows and not a tempting advertisement or decoration in sight.

It also helped that most of the town's proud architecture has survived the onslaught of war and neglect, and nineteenth-century façades and wrought-iron balconies rose above bumpy cobbled streets. Trams jingled their way around flowering squares, and park benches were busy with gossiping old men.

Originally Grudziądz was a medieval town overlooking the Vistula, and parts of the old wall remain to this day. Later innovations, such as the gas lamps that stand out from walls or atop iron lampposts, added a romantic aura to the streets. There were the crooked nooks of ancient thoroughfares to explore and, but for the cars, you were transported to another age.

The local people appeared wealthier than elsewhere and we wondered why. Perhaps the large Polish garrison outside town was a boost to business. Whatever the reason, it was the first place except Gdańsk where I would not have minded staying for a while.

Chełmno, an easy 40 kilometres further south-west, was a tiny hilltop town, its medieval character almost unchanged. A steep road curled up past the ancient watch-towers, and we were greeted by a huge main square, where a gleaming white *Rathaus* (town hall) stood in the middle.

Behind it, the inhabitants were milling about rows of market stalls, where you could buy anything from strawberries to inflatable boats.

Like in every other town, there were also people standing behind a sheet covered in old bits and pieces. Everything from shoes, pens and household goods, to obsolete medals, uniforms and identity cards were for sale. Free enterprise has really taken off on a small scale even if nationally the economy is not working. It was suggested to us that most of the vendors were Russians, come to take advantage of the stronger Polish currency.

In Berlin they say most of the hawkers are Polish or Romanian, as if it were something the locals would never do. What is certain, is that Berlin supermarkets are doing a roaring trade with Polish truck drivers. They buy up entire shelves to sell back home, especially toiletries, make-up and washing powder. (West) Berliners, meanwhile, find the shops empty when they come for their shopping and bitterly reflect that their standard of living has dropped sharply since 1989. Complaints are flowing freely from both sides of the old divide.

In a new private restaurant we met someone who had left all that behind him a long time ago.

'Are you beautiful or am I drunk?' he questioned me with a tipsy smile.

'Both,' I said, and he laughed amiably.

It was lunchtime and he had been drinking vodka all morning, enjoying himself in his old home town and boasting about his new life in Canada.

'What are you doing here?' he asked with astonishment.

It was true, there were no tourists to be seen, and we had not met any foreigners anywhere outside Gdańsk.

'What d'you mean "what are we doing here", this is a beautiful place?'

'Yes, it is,' he proudly agreed. 'It is the most beautiful little town on the Vistula. And the girls are so pretty ... But, come on, really, what are you doing here? You must know someone. No one comes here.'

He could hardly believe that foreigners would come all the way to this small town for no reason other than to simply see it and he was genuinely amazed. Frankly, we also occasionally wondered what on earth we were doing here. Poland's charm had not yet revealed itself to us very often.

Cycling through the peaceful countryside was certainly pleasant.

However, as soon as it came to finding somewhere to stay or a bite to eat we came up against regular disappointments that were already chipping away at our enthusiasm. In isolation they were trifling details, but on a daily basis they were beginning to grate. Had our encounters with people been more frequent and positive this would not have mattered. As it was, we had too much time to focus on minor frustrations.

The hotels and former workers' hostels we stayed in were almost always drab, while the meals we found there or elsewhere were regularly awful. Pizza is all the rage these days. Only the local version is usually a piece of soggy bread covered with chopped mince and cucumbers drowned in piquant ketchup. The other side of the world we would have had no expectations. But here, not far from Italy, the mushy food was disheartening. If we could have lived off ice-cream we would have had no problem at all: *lody* shops were everywhere.

Of course the traditional Polish dishes were often delicious. *Bigos*, made with sliced sausage, potatoes and cabbage with caraway was very satisfying. The trouble was finding somewhere that served it instead of the ubiquitous hamburger and chips. A poor imitation of American fast food appeared to sell better and little else was on offer.

The best-selling item of all was *piwo* (beer), and at around thirty-three US cents a bottle it was cheap and always to be found. A pretty horrible concoction, it is nevertheless drunk in enormous quantities and the inebriated people we daily saw stumbling about did nothing to make us feel less alien. It was the sheer number of alcoholics we encountered that was depressing, and the lack of self-respect.

Alcoholism was an officially sanctioned affliction under the former regime – an expedient way of keeping people's minds off the realities of their situation, and one of the most destructive legacies for the present. Not only has it left so many individuals with broken spirits, but also destroyed their most important refuge: their families. We were told that domestic violence, divorce and abandoned mothers are very common indeed.

We noticed that the majority of drunks were middle-aged and older, and very few young people were among them. With any luck the next generation will not need to dull its life with drink, but hope is not enough. Economic assistance and a genuine will among West European govern-ments to share their privileged world must be assured. If the expectations raised by 'democratic freedom' and capitalism are wholly shattered, the depth of despair and potential for violence is appalling. The cruellest trick of all is to tell a hostage he is to be set free, go through the motions, and deny it at the last moment.

'Are you beautiful or am I drunk?' asked the man for the tenth time.

At least Toruń, the last of the Teutonic settlements, left a happier impression. The town was just coming to the end of a local festival and its picturesque centre was all aflutter with colourful flags and garlands. A great tower rose above the majestic town hall and from its windy turret you could see a patchwork of red-tiled roofs spread out along the Vistula. The river was at least a hundred metres wide, and its mighty waters flowed by with daunting speed.

Great wooden barges would have docked here once, and it was the wealthy merchants of the Middle Ages who paid for the proud gabled houses that line the streets. For once we even found a good place to eat and, with a satisfied stomach and a lively atmosphere, it was easy to enjoy the place. *Dzien dobry!* (Good day) we learnt to say confidently, and people even understood us and smiled back.

THE HEART OF IT

I was still trying to get to grips with what it felt like to be in Poland. It was not altogether easy, not speaking the language, but there was more to it than that. At first I thought the alienation I felt came from being amongst people who have had to endure a system that has made them harsh to strangers and unresponsive to our smiles.

It is hard to unlearn old behaviour patterns, and the institutionalised fear that once reigned here undoubtedly forced the individual to present the outside world with a neutral face. To a far greater extent than crowds ignore each other in the West, it was necessary here to be as invisible as possible; to remain unnoticed and unnoticing. Most people never get over the hang-ups of their youth, so why should Poles be able to switch into a more open and spontaneous way of being after a whole lifetime of repression? Why, too, should they welcome their privileged European 'brothers and sisters', whose governments have so far failed to put their money where their mouths are? Understandable enough, but it did not make for pleasant company.

At least young people should find it easier. But they, in turn, cannot automatically shake off their parents' upbringing and must also have a struggle on their hands. It is just like Philip Larkin said: 'Man hands on misery to man, It deepens like a coastal shelf.' The apathy of a society so recently used to total control still hangs in the air and spoils the atmosphere, in spite of Solidarity's heroic efforts.

Yet this was not quite enough to explain my underlying feeling of being out of Europe, far from what *I* knew, at least, as European culture. Could it be that the common ground I was looking for was not so easily found because Poland does not share the same cultural heritage as, say, England, France or Germany? After all, this is a Slav country. Many of its regions and significant numbers of its people have a tradition that is tied closer to Moscow and the Orthodox faith than to any Western capital or the Vatican. True, Poland is staunchly Catholic now, but Orthodox Christians have lived within the country's shifting territory ever since the fourteenth century, while the thirteenth-century Tartar invasions resulted in a Muslim minority remaining ever since. The country's fortunes and culture have been characterised by dominance from the East for hundreds of years.

The origins of its society lie with the Slavonic Empire that grew up on the eastern frontier of Charlemagne's Frankish domain, and the ninth-century borderlands, which were in present-day Moravia, were almost the same as the Roman ones before them. (Brno, the capital of Moravia, was the most north-easterly Roman outpost.) The cultural and political traditions of Poland have never been the same as the ones of Western Europe. This may be ancient history, yet its effect is real enough.

It was the Romans who first developed the tempting fiction of a unified (European) empire, and while that idea has been thoroughly discredited, the illusion of a unified confederate Europe, including East and West European countries, is still alive and well. In fact, this Europe never existed, and the Iron Curtain was not so much a division, as the temporary re-establishment of an ancient divide in a region that has been fragmented since the collapse of the early pan-European empires. What has blandly been called 'Eastern Europe' is actually a puzzle of national-ities, languages and cultures with profound regional differences in politi-cal and economic development which are far greater than in 'Western Europe'. There is no reason at all to think they can match up into any kind of homogeneous entity, let alone that all European countries could blend in together.

Perhaps it was the Slav flavour of Poland that gave me such a strong sense of being in an altogether other world. Even the language sounded Russian to me, and people explained that they could understand not only Russian, but also much of the Serbian and Macedonian languages. Their common roots are undeniably strong.

How to explain the intangible sense of otherness? It is a way people look at each other in the street: straight in the eye, unswerving, yet blank. At the same time there is an archaic formality that I can only compare to the older generation of Germans or French. Men still commonly greet female acquaintances with a hand kiss, and they address each other 'Sir' or 'Madam'. Even young people can be surprisingly formal, and it happened to me once that a woman my own age shook hands with me and curtsied.

I am not saying that I did not like Poland. Only that it was undeniably strange to me in a way no Western European country could have been. Our historic trade route was taking us close to an ancient social fault line and even being an atheist and ignorant of the historic facts, I could certainly *feel* it.

Maybe the reason for my unease was much simpler. It is possible that exposure to West European culture and history through schooling, television and travel created a subconscious familiarity and my plain ignorance of any East European country inevitably made a first encounter feel like an awkward meeting of strangers. The very word 'Europe' had misled me to presume I would automatically find a cultural rapport in Poland, where otherwise I would have had no expectations.

I suspected that I would not feel like this in Czecho-Slovakia or Hungary, since they were once controlled by the Austro-Hungarian Empire, a Western power, even if many of its people to the east had a separate cultural heritage. The Czechs and Slovaks are also Slavs, while the Hungarians are Magyars, with an entirely different ancestry and linguistic background to any other Central or East European nation.

On the other hand, the Polish and Czech crown were once the same, under Wenceslas II, and even Hungary was briefly added to his family's domain, when Wenceslas's son was offered the Hungarian crown after the local Árpád dynasty died out in 1301. In fact, these three countries came under the same crown at various times in the Middle Ages. Yet people had already told us repeatedly 'don't go to Czecho-Slovakia', displaying a knee-jerk dislike for their neighbours. Which parts of history mattered for today? I would have to wait and see.

Serbia and Macedonia would no doubt be another experience altogether. Southern Slavs, their history and culture are stamped not only by Tsarist influences and the Orthodox Church, but also by Islamic Turkish domination right up until the nineteenth century. No doubt cultural communality would be difficult to find there too.

History and religion are stronger influences than modern political delineations, something I was finding out firsthand already. The war in former Yugoslavia bears this out. Intellectuals may have mixed freely from Barcelona to Kraków, St Petersburg to London. Their common ground, however, was not in culture but in learning.

Beyond the last Teutonic stronghold of Toruń we finally entered the historic heart of Poland, that ancient region known as Wielkopolska (Great Poland), where the Polish State was first born, and to Gniezno, its first capital. It was here, in what is now western Poland, that the legend of the country's birth took shape, and it is still an important location today – not politically, but as the ecclesiastical capital.

According to legend, the Slav brothers Lech, Czech and Rus were the founders of the Polish, Czech and Ruthenian (forebears of the Ukrainian) nations. Each chose a different region for his people, and Lech made his choice when he found the nest (*gniazdo*) of a uniquely white eagle. From that day on, he ruled the Polanians from his capital in Gniezno, and the eagle was chosen as the emblem for what was to become Poland. That is the folklore. Known as historic fact, is that a tribal chief of the Polanians, called Miesko I, founded the Piast dynasty some time in the tenth century, whose kingdom spread out from this original heartland. Bolesław the Brave, Miesko's son, became the first King of Poland, crowned by the German Emperor, Otto III, in the year 1000.

Gniezno lost its position as Polish capital as long ago as 1038 and, in spite of remaining home to the nation's archbishop, is now a small provincial town. The only people who come here are a steady stream of pilgrims to the local cathedral, which makes it almost impossible to find cheap accommodation, and we were lucky to gain access to a workers' hostel beyond the train station.

A pot-holed cobbled road led us over the railway tracks and the station's sidings, where a yard stood filled with locomotives. They were painted in strident yellow, green and orange, and their fifties design conjured up images of the jolly engine characters from old cartoons. No doubt they would soon be for the scrap heap, replaced by sleek trains capable of modern speeds, which seemed a shame. But old-fashioned machines are only romantic if you do not have to depend on them, and the locals probably can't wait to see them relegated, though they might keep some for their museums.

We, however, had not come here to see the cathedral or visit museums, but because Gniezno is more or less on the amber trail. Evidence for this comes from one of the most ancient sources available, in the shape of a prehistoric village 30 kilometres north, called Biskupin. The whole region is peppered with these settlements, only this one is superbly preserved on a former island in a small lake.

Due to lower water levels, what was once an island is now part of a mini peninsula of around five acres, and a short walk across marshy ground brings you to the village entrance. The surrounding bog is an excellent conserver for all kinds of matter, and not only have large sections of the fortifications survived for over two thousand years, but so have other traces of the society that lived here. Pottery, bone and bronze tools and amulets, human burials and, of course, amber beads and pendants have been found, many dating back to 550 BC, when Biskupin was built. Roman coins dating from the first centuries also show that the descendants of Biskupin's founders were closely associated with the amber trade route that emerged at that time.

The people who once lived here were members of the Lusation culture, whose history spanned over two millenia, from the Middle Bronze Age (1200 BC onwards) to the early Middle Ages. Their settlements have been discovered in many parts of Europe, reaching as far west as German Saxony. Communities of up to one thousand people led a simple pastoral life, gathering herbs, nuts and fruit from the surrounding forests, cultivating cereals, and keeping cattle and pigs, as well as smaller animals, such as sheep, goats and dogs. They lived in long houses, each about nine metres long, and divided into two rooms: one main room for living and sleeping in, and a hall the length of the entire building for storage and keeping animals. The whole family slept together, which would have meant up to twelve bodies in the same bed.

That they had contact with other peoples is evidenced by finds of artifacts from far away, such as glass beads from Egypt, that reached them via the Balkans, bronze from Transylvania, iron tools from Silesia, amber from the Baltic, and many objects from neighbouring regions, such as Bohemia and Hungary.

Distant connections are also recognised by common artistic styles or imitations of foreign designs. For example, some patterns on pottery from early Slav tribes are similar to Minoan art from Crete, which suggests there were links between the Baltic and Aegean as early as the sixteenth century BC, long before Biskupin existed. The most striking piece of evidence comes from an archaeological site in Bohemia, where a clay cup is believed to be an imitation of a Minoan gold and silver vessel, known as the Vapheio cup.

The seasonal journeys for pasture, as well as periodic migrations brought the earliest contacts, and it was these routes that eventually also became the established arteries of trade. Further routes were forged when tribes migrated far away from their homeland, yet still required certain items for their particular way of life. For example, one of the first objects to be carried long distances, which can only have happened by human hand, was shell. Specifically shells from the Black Sea, which have been found in prehistoric sites as far north and west as Poland and Germany, and were probably used for tools and ornamental purposes. Just like anyone else, early societies liked to keep to their traditional way of life and went to great lengths to get supplies of the things they wanted.

So how was trade done in those days? Clearly, words like barter and exchange are better descriptions, since money is a relatively recent invention, but there are a number of different kinds of transactions that probably took place. One would have been annual visits to specific sites, where a particular tool or ornament was found, the supply of which was controlled by a different, resident tribe. This kind of trade can still be found among aboriginal people today, where representatives of distinct tribes will travel long distances to gather and exchange goods. Another kind of early trade was possibly established by travelling 'merchants', who maintained seasonal trading posts that were visited by remote peoples, though it is doubtful whether these posts existed in prehistoric times. Indisputably, however, exchange of goods was the path to trade, and this in turn generated demand for luxuries. Thus the early civilisations of south-eastern Europe sent their bronze tools to the distant north, and their couriers returned with important raw materials, such as tin from Cornwall, but also Baltic amber for ornamentation, healing and religious ritual. (In spite of the direction I chose to travel in, it must be said that the first contacts are believed to have been made by southern tribes heading north and eastern tribes heading west, rather than the other way round.)

The traditional paths between the Baltic and the southern cultures of the Black Sea, Adriatic and Aegean were established following river valleys and low mountain passes where travel on foot and with animals was easiest. At first, goods were either carried or dragged on sliding sledges, later to be replaced by wheeled carts. The people of Biskupin, for example, already used the wheel, and large disc wheels of solid oak have been found in the bog around the village. Horses were also kept, and they were used both for riding and as pack animals, though sturdy oxen would have been more common for pulling heavy weights. Sometimes the rivers themselves would be used, either by travelling in skin boats stretched over a wooden hull, or in dug-out canoes. The latter have survived quite well, and have been found in archaeological sites all over Europe.

River travel is hard to prove, however, and it is much easier to show where overland routes existed. This is not only because of the intermittent hoards of goods that have been found, but also because timber trackways were laid down to make paths easier to travel on. Remains of these have survived right up to the present, and Biskupin is one of the places where traces can still be found.

The builders of Biskupin devised a clever protective design for their village by driving a series of oak stakes into the ground all around the island's shore. There were several layers of these, at an angle of forty-five degrees, similar to the serried rows of sharks' teeth. Behind them was built a six-metre high wall of oak and pine, strengthened by boxed earth and sand on the inside, where sentries kept strategic piles of stones to pelt invaders. Anyone approaching could be seen easily, since there was just one gateway through the ramparts, approached by a log causeway raised above the water and connecting with the mainland, about 120 metres away. This causeway was, of course, just the last stretch of a much longer track, that would have led to the most commonly travelled destinations visited by Biskupin residents and other travellers.

Inside the fortifications stood thirteen rows of wooden long houses thatched with reed, and what makes visiting Biskupin so interesting is that the Polish authorities have rebuilt two of these houses as they once were. Wandering about their windowless interiors, you get a real sense of what Iron Age life was like. Fireplaces and tools are on display in their proper places, and there are even women, dressed in sackcloth and moccasins, weaving on traditional looms. The effect is excellent, enlivening the ancient past in a way no history book can.

★

'Pylons, factories and chimneys,' grumbled Benoît. 'All Polish towns are exactly the same.'

He was right. Virtually all the towns we had passed so far had a fuming ring of industry, followed by a barricade of faceless housing blocks, which hid a small historic centre gathered around the church. Paved roads and twentieth-century technology held each place in deadly embrace, choking a withering heart of crumbling buildings that spanned the last five centuries or more.

'I'm so sick of this flat countryside,' he sulked.

I had to admit that Poland's monotonous flatness really was getting boring, even if my thighs were grateful for it. Cycling through leafy arcades of country roads, occasionally passing under the gaze of storks, and watching the endless sea of poppies flutter in the breeze was still a pleasure – but wearing a bit thin after a couple of weeks. What was more, the towns did all blend into one after a while, and I soon gave up taking out my camera. One medieval town square looked much like another, and I knew already that it would be difficult to remember which picture came from where back home.

I tried to be positive to rally Benoît's spirits and encourage his enthusiasm, but he was clearly getting bored and I became plagued by the thought that he might decide to leave, go home, or head off somewhere else. Now that I was not travelling alone, the idea of being left was a worrying one.

My friends have occasionally taunted me: 'Ha, if people could see you now, so small and uncertain. Is this the same woman who went down the Amazon alone?' It was as if having done something they considered unthinkably brave I was supposed to be impervious to insecurity or fear. Because I had always been a solo traveller they imagined I must be very strong and never have doubts or feel vulnerable, never need the comfort of a friend. There is no such person, and bravery has to do with overcoming fear. For me it would be incredibly brave to go parachuting because I hate flying and am terrified of falling. My journeys had nothing to do with bravery because I was not scared of them, only of specific situations.

Yet now I was scared, scared that Benoît would leave me to my crazy project just when I had settled in to being in company, having a partner to share things with and not having to rely completely on my own resources.

(Who else would pump air into my tires?!) I could not even cycle as fast or as long as him, and he was getting frustrated with that too. At times I resented him. Hadn't I said a thousand times this journey was not for speed, but to find out something, find answers to questions?

On the other hand I understood his complaints. This was not his project. He was along for the ride, for the fun, and it was not fun at the moment. Being Canadian, the prospect of a new Europe did not hold the same excitement for him, and what were burning questions for me were nothing but interesting topics that did not touch him personally. His commitment was to me and not my ideas and he was not automatically wild about joining me wherever they took me. I had to respect that. But, however unreasonable, I could not help wishing for a bit more support. If we were going to be a team I wanted equal dedication.

Yet as a couple we were well tuned and instinctively gave each other the space to level out. In the end I could not deny that Poland did seem disappointing and no matter how much I tried to be enthusiastic, our experiences clearly stared us in the face.

We reached Poznań (Posen) soon after Gniezno, the first large city since Gdańsk, and we looked forward to enjoying the cultural and social attractions of this proud city. But our hearts sank when we saw placards announcing the annual trade fair, guaranteed to send all prices rocketing beyond our reach. Youth or student hostels would be the most affordable we reasoned, and tried the first listed in our guidebook. It was shut, and not for the first time we cursed the author for sloppy research. (In Toruń the youth hostel had turned out to be a derelict building.) No matter. Some helpful taxi-drivers pointed us towards student hostels the other side of the city, and we pedalled off to find them.

A busy road took us up and up and into a suburb of tower blocks and concrete. The hostels were indistinguishable from other blocks on the estate, and when at last we found them, a surly concierge insisted on a price five times above the usual. It was an absurd rip-off and, being in no mood to pay through the nose, we abandoned Poznań without much ado. A look at the map showed that our route south offered no particular excitement, so we took a train to the city of Wrocław (Breslau) instead, speeding through yet more flat countryside.

It was definitely time for a cycling break and we arranged to deposit our bikes in Wrocław, leaving its discovery for later. For now we travelled to Kraków, the country's most famous city and one of Europe's oldest cultural centres. This was Poland's capital for over five hundred years before being superseded by Warsaw after 1596, and its university was founded as early as the fourteenth century. It is a place rich in historic glamour and human achievement, with a reputation for freedom and tolerance, in spite of the Holocaust that emptied many of its homes in the early 1940s and the subsequent repression of another regime.

Yet, more strikingly than any other city, Kraków also fits the national pattern of being smothered by industry. About sixty kilometres before Kraków the train from Wrocław reaches one of the worst environmental catastrophes in Europe: the Katowice conurbation, where thin poles of aluminium chimneys send pollution into the sky like the smouldering trunks of a burning forest. It is a monstrous vision of industrial hell that is only surpassed by one of the largest European steelworks on the outskirts of Kraków itself: Nowa Huta.

It was the communist determination to give this seditiously intellectual and Catholic city a proletarian hue that caused the horror, and both people and architecture are suffering badly. Respiratory and skin diseases, as well as birth defects are abnormally common, while the lovely medieval and renaissance buildings carry the green-black stain of acid rain. Kraków has the distinction of being both on UNESCO's list of world historic monuments and Greenpeace's list of the world's ecological disaster areas.

The country is on its knees and it is no surprise that few migrants trying to enter Western Europe from the east and south are stopping off here. The majority of foreign residents we saw were here because they had been brought in by the old system: Russian soldiers or Vietnamese guest workers, and a smattering of African students from former allies, like Ethiopia. The only other group of foreigners are the Gypsies, mostly from Romania, who have fled in droves from the persecution and poverty in their traditional homeland.

Perhaps because of the greater number of tourists, Kraków also had a large clan of Gypsies residing in its streets. Their daytime encampment was outside the railway station where we too were staying, in a hotel opposite. The barefoot women sat in a garrulous cluster on some grass, sorting out crumpled clothes and untangling their occasionally fighting children. They seemed to carry most of their wardrobe on their bodies, one skirt over another, blouses and cardigans layered on top, and always wearing a traditional headscarf. The picture-book costume of folklore had long been lost to poverty and an itinerant life offering no respite for craftwork any more. Their bare skin was encrusted with dirt and it was easy to see why they inspired fear and prejudice.

Yet they were distinct from other 'vagrants' in that they still seemed to have a clear code of behaviour, and remained in their clan. They were not sad, lonely people. While the women were busy with the children and begging, the men sat under the shade of a tree, keeping a patriarchal eye on them. They were smart compared to their women, more often than not wearing a trilby kind of hat, matching trousers and jacket, and always shoes on their feet. I never saw them actually do anything, though they undoubtedly had some kind of business.

The glitzy shops that have sprung up in Kraków's elegant centre were in stark contrast to everything we had seen around it. Here were jazz cafés, wine bars, fashion shops with anything from Dior to Benetton, and a crowd that looked wealthy enough to buy whatever it desired. The huge main square – the largest in medieval Europe – was lined by immaculately restored buildings, their fine arches and gables an elegant setting for the pedestrian life they looked on to.

Some Bolivians played jerky Andean rhythms on their pan flutes, captivating many listeners. They seemed strangely out of place in their ponchos and wool hats, but no more so than the huge balloon being fired up in another corner of the square. Expectant shoppers waited patiently until the giant contraption rose at last, and a hundred chins followed its course above the rooftops. A tiny couple waved from the dangling basket, releasing a shower of leaflets, which turned out to be for nothing less mundane than a German make of gas boiler. Elsewhere, drunks were gathered oblivious around a statue, sharing the benches with hopeful young men clutching single red roses.

There was a myriad of attractions to fill hours of wandering about, and centre stage was taken up by a grand rectangular cloth hall with an Aladdin's cave of trinket and craft shops selling everything from plastic dolls to exquisite Polish lace. On the flagstones outside clustered flower vendors with fragrant buckets, and beyond them the stalls of a second-hand market. The city was home to one of the largest Jewish communities in Europe for 600 years, and some of the more macabre items for sale were old identity cards stamped with the Star of David and the official Nazi swastika underneath. Dog-eared copies of *Mein Kampf* were also quite frequent and I dreaded to think what kind of people would wish to buy these horrible relics.

You would think that the reign of terror that once stalked these streets would have left some kind of lingering atmosphere, but it is only the imagination that can create that. The lovely buildings offer no hint of what they have seen. The cobbled drive sweeping up Wawel Hill to the royal enclave of castle and cathedral could as well resound to the hooves of noble carriages as to the slap of army boots, and in a sense even the smallest knowledge of history clouds one's impression of this glamorous place.

The view over Kraków's great mansions and medieval outline is the most impressive aspect of Wawel Hill. The buildings inside the fortifications are almost an anti-climax by comparison and they look better on the approach than face to face. The most memorable part of the castle for me was the exterior, which was rebuilt to Italian design, with a courtyard framed by two tiers of slender arches and ivy growing decoratively up the walls. The neighbouring cathedral is a painful mix of architectural styles ranging from Byzantine gold-plated cupolas to Gothic gargoyles. Inside, the variety of design is even more chaotic, and its proud history and sacred place in the nation's heart helps little to create the awe it should inspire.

We left the votive and candlestick sellers to stroll along the banks of the Vistula. When we had last seen her at Toruń she was a mighty river heading towards the sea. Here her waters were younger and narrower, but still impressive, washing the base of Wawel Hill before curving around the old Jewish quarter of Kazimierz. The predominantly nineteenth-century apartment blocks show few signs of the society that once lived here. Yet free enterprise is doing good business with 'Jewish Tours of Kraków' and air-conditioned buses leave daily for Oświęcim (Auschwitz), which lies an hour west of the city. Posters offered day trips with an English-speaking guide for an obnoxious US$70. The train fare cost less than US$10 and there are no words that can enhance the horror of a place like Auschwitz.

Certainly for me, the magnitude of what happened here is beyond my comprehension. As usual I found myself confused by what I could see and the scraps of history I knew. What I saw were neat rows of oblong,

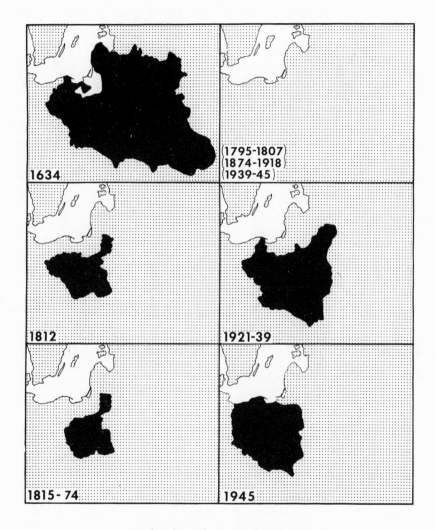

Poland's Changing Territory
From: *Heart of Europe*, Norman Davies, OUP, 1991 (paperback).

redbrick houses and tidy gravel paths lined by poplar trees. Birds twittered on the roofs and I wondered if they had done so fifty years ago.

What has always staggered me most – whether in the remote Andes or in a building that has witnessed unspeakable acts – is that the material and natural world remains unmoved by the fate of people. The manner of human life or death leaves no mark except in our minds and that frightens me most of all. Millions died here (about four million), but if it was not for the mountains of spectacles, shoes, baby clothing and suitcases on display, you would never know it. I wish I could take comfort in the belief that there is a point to everything. This place only confirmed for me once more that there is no point to anything except the one people create for themselves.

There is a black-and-white film shot by the Russian liberators which peoples the empty site with the tragic faces of 1945. In Thomas Keneally's *Schindler's Ark* a woman recognises her child in this film and I wondered which one it was – if that detail is true, which I hope it is.

We visited the camp on the way back to Wrocław, and the silent hours on the train helped ease our minds back into the present. Both of us were ready to hit the road now, and we looked forward to the challenge of our first serious hills. Soon we would be climbing into the Sudeten mountains that form part of the natural border between Poland and Czecho-Slovakia, and already the anticipation was lifting our spirits.

Towards the Kłodzko Pass

'I don't feel like going to bed,' said Benoît.

It was only 10 p.m., yet wandering around Wrocław's centre earlier on, we had found the streets almost empty by suppertime. The main square had been eerily quiet, with only the occasional laugh or clatter of shoes to break the silence. It was a weekend in late June, but the cafés and open-air beer tables had already been cleared away, and after Kraków this place felt very subdued. Few tourists were here to enliven commerce and the locals seemed to have neither the money nor the habit for socialising in public.

Setting off to find the city's nightlife did not hold much promise in these circumstances, and the liveliest place appeared to be the train station, where kiosks were open late into the night. As usual we were staying nearby in the cheap hotels, and so decided to head that way first.

As I came out of the hotel entrance I saw a man lying on the street. He was flat on his back with his arms outstretched, a short distance from a bus. A crowd stood around him. Someone tried to feel his pulse. Someone else fingered his neck, and then a woman broke in to pound his chest. She jumped on his body and pummelled madly, as if trying to revitalise him with sheer rage against fate. But the man remained unmoving except when touched, his body still warm and malleable.

It was an age before an ambulance arrived. Had anyone called one? But there were two policemen taking statements from the bus passengers, and it seemed the situation must be in hand. The accident had happened on a busy junction, and traffic converging from four directions was rapidly becoming turgid with gawping drivers and pedestrians.

Finally a car with a red cross on it arrived and parked next to the man on the crossroads. Someone put a towel over his face, since it was obvious by now that he was past saving. There was almost no blood, but a head-size dent on the side of the bus showed how hard the impact had been. At least, we assured each other, he must have died instantly.

Meanwhile the ambulance men did nothing except put a black plastic bag over the corpse and move their vehicle on to the nearest pavement. A carful of policemen arrived, who proceeded to move onlookers off the street and take control of the traffic. The body, still lying beside the bus, was increasingly stepped over by busy officials, his plastic outline reflecting the changing colours of the traffic lights. He was a lonely sight, lying there surrounded by people and heaving traffic, and we wondered how long he would have to lie there unattended.

At last a larger ambulance came, at least half an hour later, and orderlies in white coats stepped out with a large case. 'Now they'll take him away,' we told each other, magnetised by the scene as much as anyone. But no. The orderlies simply confirmed the death and drove off within minutes of arrival, leaving the body like discarded rubbish on the wayside. He was only a stiff, not a person with feelings, and no dignity was spared him now. Police cars and uniformed men increased in number, but nothing happened. The busiest man was an official measuring the scene of the accident with a white marker. He pushed a small trolley, like the kind to mark tennis lawns, drawing white lines and measuring angles.

In the meantime a blue light and siren announced another arrival, this time the photographer – for the police or press we could not tell. He took flash photos from all angles: of the bus, the dent and the victim. He drew back the bin-liner to record the face and wound close-up. Once finished, he stood chatting with a policeman by the feet, while all around them wardens were trying to direct cars against the indications on the traffic lights. Confused drivers alternately jammed on the brakes or drove through a stop whistle, distracted by conflicting messages and the crowd.

The chaos contrasted sharply with the lifeless shape on the tarmac, and it was grotesque the way the dead man seemed to have no importance whatsoever, other than as a piece of evidence. It was an hour before the hearse arrived – an estate car with makeshift curtains – and only after the police, the photographer and others had exchanged handshakes and pleasantries, was the body at last made ready for moving.

The final indignity came when he was searched for his I.D. and valuables. Someone lifted his limp fingers to remove the rings, another unclipped a gold necklace from his neck, and then the contents of his shirt and trouser pockets was emptied into a paper bag. His head flopped over on to a contorted hand when they turned him on his side, and he looked uncomfortably asleep. Finally they rolled him on to a blanket and heaved him into the back of the hearse, and that was that.

All this time the woman who had pounded the man's chest stood on the pavement nearby, ignored and unquestioned. Now she left with two friends, all of them unsteady on their feet, and I realised for the first time that the dead man and his friends were alcoholics, their bout rudely interrupted by this accident. One companion shoved a vodka bottle at the woman, as if to say 'have a drink', but she stalked off ahead, unsteady but purposeful. Would she remember how she had lost her partner? Would anyone bother to tell her where he was to be buried? It seemed unlikely.

The victim was a drunk and perhaps that was the reason why he had been left lying about for so long. His killing seemed to rate little more than a dog's, and when the scene cleared, even the bus driver was free to drive off, apparently uncharged. Only a small puddle of blood marked the recent loss of life, and oblivious car tyres quickly spread it into wet tracks on the road.

Cosseted from death in our own culture, it was hard to digest this nonchalant treatment of human fatality. We associated what we had seen with the Third World, where death is a daily and public fact of life. Here in Poland we found it disturbingly brutal. Yet soon we too had put the event out of our minds – after all, he was a stranger – and sat drinking cans of beer with more of his kind in the station.

On closer inspection Wrocław (pronounced Fvrots-waf) does have its attractions, set as it is on the banks of the Odra River. A series of stone bridges offer beautiful views of the city, characterised by proud Gothic spires rising above the roofs of medieval and renaissance buildings and grand nineteenth-century apartments along the river. This is extraordinary when you consider that up to 70 per cent of the city was demolished by fighting in 1945, and the people of Wrocław have rebuilt the city almost from scratch.

I would say 'their city', only 75 per cent of the original German population fled or was deported, replaced by displaced Poles from what is now the Ukraine. What was once called Breslau (from 1526 to 1945) is now Wrocław, and yet earlier still (from 1335 to 1526), it was known as Vraclav, when it was part of the Czech Bohemian Kingdom.

★

Just when we had decided travelling in Poland was disappointing, we had a number of friendly encounters that tempered our impressions, while the countryside transformed itself into a pre-alpine landscape of forested hills and picturesque valleys. As we cycled into the Sudeten mountains, the tower blocks and fumes of industrial Silesia were left behind and the acrid smell of burning coal gave way to the fresh air of forests and dewy pastures. Hilltop towns huddled behind ancient fortifications, and young rivers swept over mossy boulders in churning waterfalls.

We cycled an energetic 72 kilometres from Wrocław to Paczków, passing small villages and tumbledown churchyards where willow trees brushed sunken tombstones. The farms in this region were quite different to others we had seen so far. No longer small redbrick structures, or wooden either, they were fine two-storey houses surrounded by a yard of large stone barns and arched stable-doors. Once they must have been proud country estates, now sadly derelict, still waiting for a new lease of life. For some of them it was obviously too late, and itinerant families of Gypsies were stripping every last floorboard and rafter for firewood.

In the small town of Ziębice we ate the usual sausage and chips with a warm lemonade, and sat dazed in the oppressive heat. The weather was unusually humid, and our bare legs stuck uncomfortably to plastic seats. We decided to rest for a while behind the church. It was the only place we could find cool grass and a shading tree, and we lay exhausted on the ground. Gazing empty-headed through the branches, it was good to feel the bones and muscles of my back and hips gradually relax.

Soon old heads were eyeing us from window-sills, cushions conveniently placed for elbows, and I hoped we were not causing offence. An old lady in her traditional housewife's smock came ambling past and stopped to chat. 'Where are you from?' she seemed to say, and I explained we were English. She pointed to the bikes, and I nodded to her obvious question. '*Tak*' (Yes), I said, and listed the main towns since Gdańsk, while she nodded ever more enthusiastic. Her curiosity satisfied she continued on her way, but before long another woman came out to inspect us.

'*Bitte trinken*' (Please drink), she said in German, and held out a large jar of piping hot red liquid which turned out to be home-made cherry juice. It was delicious, and she insisted that we drink as much as we could and put the rest into our water-bottles. She clucked and gasped when I told her where we had come from, scuttling back and forth to tell her husband, who was keeping his distance behind the curtains. Soon she was asking us to stay with her, and it was touching to be treated like long-lost grandchildren. Alas, we had already set our hearts on reaching the border as soon as possible and declined her kind offer with handshakes and grateful smiles.

Later on, that day, I had another impromptu German conversation. We had stopped to pump up our tyres when a weather-beaten old man on a bicycle pulled up beside us. He was looking for a tool shop, but was in no hurry to find it, wrapping me in a long conversation. He was from Lvov, former capital of the Polish Ukraine, and full of yarns about his days as a soldier. He had fought only briefly, and spent most of his time a prisoner of war somewhere near Hannover where he had picked up German, and he was pleased how much he could remember, even after all this time.

'*Die haben grosse Schweinerei gemacht*' (They've got a lot to answer for), he said of Hitler and company.

He had spent almost five years building underground bunkers for the Germans, and once was moved by train to another camp. Many froze to death in transit but their captors had painted *Korn Transport* on the wagons, and left the rest with the corpses until darkness had fallen.

'Now everything is bad again,' he hummed, 'the zloty was worth one Deutschmark in the old days. Now everything is very expensive and there is no work ... *Die Kommunisten haben grosse Schweinerei gemacht*' (The communists have a lot to answer for), he said, using his favourite expression. 'History repeats itself even in one lifetime, and we are no better off.'

He clasped my hand with knobbly fingers and reluctantly bade us farewell. His grandchildren had probably heard his stories *ad nauseam*. But we were glad to have met him, and I almost wished we could have stayed to hear more.

In Paczków at last, we decided to camp, and found a very pleasant site completely empty. There was even a swimming-pool, and the town was a charming place clustered around a cobbled square and ancient watch-towers standing guard in the old wall. By dusk we were drinking draught beer among raucous men and women on the main square, where a colour television was showing the semi-final for the European Cup.

Beer mugs slammed on to the table-tops, roars of approval came with every good move and, almost for the first time, we felt at ease among strangers. I care neither for beer nor for football, but the atmosphere in this smoky bar was easy-going and the people around us seemed to have a sense of fun and tolerance that ran deeper than alcohol.

After Paczków the cycling got much tougher as we headed south-west, into the Kłodzko valley that lead up to the Kłodzko Pass (Glatz Pass) and the Czech border. It was so hazy we could hardly see the hills around us, but we certainly felt them, and I had to get off and push twice. My legs were as fit as could be, but the weight on the back of the bicycle put any incline over eight degrees beyond me. The downhills were wonderful, though, wind drying the sweat on our faces and a cool breeze blowing around our steaming bodies. I never knew I could drink so much, but I easily downed a couple of litres of water while cycling. We had three large bottles between us, and even these were not enough sometimes.

On one particularly fast descent I suddenly heard a loud crack from my back wheel and my heart jumped as I almost lost control. Something had smashed into a hundred pieces and fallen off behind me, yet when I examined the bike I could see nothing wrong. The wheel was fine and the spokes were all in place, and it was only when I walked up the road that I realised I had had a lucky escape: the reflector that had been attached to the rear wheel spokes had caught on a strap or hook and snapped off into the spinning wheel. I must have been going around thirty miles an hour at the time and I shuddered to think what might have happened.

Meanwhile Benoît had long shot out of sight, and by the time we met up he was retracing his steps with horrible anticipation. A truck driver had indicated that he should turn back, but he had not stopped to speak, and for all Benoît knew I or my bike was lying mangled on the roadside. Happily no harm was done, and it was a good lesson in the importance of checking our bikes each day. Already we had lost a few nuts and screws that had worked themselves loose on the cobblestones, but we had still not got into the habit of attending to our machines. Neither of us is mechanically minded and we were much too prone to hope for the best instead of careful maintenance.

Safely over our first ridge of hills, however, we glided into the bustling town of Kłodzko, which gives the valley its name, and found ourselves transported into the Tyrolean atmosphere of a faded spa town. A medieval stone bridge led over an icy river to the base of the old centre, and a small square busy with market stalls. The town was built on tiers up a steep riverbank, and narrow streets looped up and around fine buildings with wooden shutters and wrought-iron balconies. It was a good place for a rest and a snack, but then we pressed onwards, reaching Bystrzyca just in time before the air was cleared by a heavy rainstorm.

By now the valley had narrowed considerably, and the fortified town was squeezed on a ledge above the confluence of two mountain rivers. Pine trees clung precariously to moist cliffs, roots dangling, and there was a refreshing smell of damp wood and moss. Inside the medieval walls, crumbling arches and narrow alleys hid two squares awash from broken drainpipes that sent us skipping among the torrents. It was a relief to find a hotel in this rain where we could have a hot shower and dry our clothes.

Tomorrow, we had already decided, we were going to cheat and take a train to the last town before the border. We imagined it would be uphill all the way and Benoît was persuaded to ease the challenge. There was no escaping the last 7 kilometres to the pass, however, and I was dreading it.

Next morning we peered through steamed-up windows as our train snaked along the base of the valley, and all too soon we pulled in to our final stop and had to make ready for cycling in the rain. Clouds sat milky white on the treetops, and as our bikes traced a shiny line on the wet tarmac, my thoughts drifted off to the ancient past.

I took satisfaction in knowing that we were travelling on the very same path that migrants and traders had taken from time immemorial. As long ago as the Bronze Age, well over a thousand years before Christ, men and women began using this route to cross the Sudeten mountains before reaching the Moravian plain and the Morava River leading to the Danube. This was the connection between the peoples of the Vistula basin and northern Baltic, and the Danubians, who were in touch with the myriad of cultures that lay in every direction from their homeland.

To the east along the Danube, they came to the Black Sea settlements, whose people had their own trade routes to yet more distant places, such as Asia. To the south-west, there were established routes via modern Slovenia towards the Adriatic and North Africa. Directly south, along the rivers we were to follow, was the way to the Aegean, and some of the earliest civilisations, such as the Greeks, and the Phoenicians, who were based along the coast of modern Syria. They too were linked to other cultures by a web of further trade routes, in particular with the Middle East.

It is no wonder then, that you can find goods and imitations of artistic styles from people living at opposite ends of the European mainland, even from thousands of years ago. It is easy to think that primitive people in sackcloth and furs could not possibly have known about other cultures beyond their horizon. Perhaps they did not. In any event they did not need to, because the combination of migrations, barter and trade between neighbouring people could just as easily lead to goods and ideas travelling long distances without the originators ever meeting the recipients.

A prime example is the Baltic amber that reached the early Greeks. It is clear that they had no accurate knowledge of where it came from, how it was formed or gathered, and yet they had use for it. Even the Romans were at first unclear on where exactly amber came from and, since they valued it so highly, sent spies to find out.

They also used this method to find the source of another highly valued commodity: tin, which was crucial for making bronze. The early Romans believed tin came from the legendary isles of the Cassiterides, in reality Cornwall. But seafaring merchants did everything they could to keep the true source a secret, and there is even a story of a merchant sinking his ship rather than letting a Roman vessel trace his contacts.

This mountain pass then, was our first crucial marker on the amber trail – one of the few places that I knew with absolute certainty was on the route. For the longest time there must have been a muddy track rutted by horses and ox-drawn carts, and I was glad to be simply pedalling on a smooth road. We moved slowly uphill, through the rain, but protected by plastic and knowing that we would find food and shelter by nightfall.

In fact, the pass was easy to reach. It was only 540 metres high and the road leading to the Polish side rose gently past meadows and pine trees. For a time we wondered if we had missed the border altogether, until a small building became visible through the mist. It was a pity not to see more of this important landmark, but it remained shrouded in a watery haze. Only the faintest outline of trees and houses was visible, and we cycled into Czecho-Slovakia laced up to our noses, eyes blinking against the rain.

For the first time I even put my plastic leggings on, explaining to Benoît that cold and wet almost always gave me rheumatic knees.

'This is the intrepid traveller!' he snorted, and cycled off.

But I was quickly tailing his back wheel, both of us suddenly raring to go. The miserable weather teased our imagination, withholding views of the new country, and we could hardly wait to reach the first town.

2. CZECHO-SLOVAKIA

To them [Central and Eastern Europeans], *the medieval period means much more than it means to Western nations. It was then that most of them came nearest to their ideals of national independence . . . And when their national individuality was adsorbed into the neighbouring empires of Germany, Austria, Muscovite Russia and Ottoman Turkey, it was from those memories that they drew comfort and strength. Today, their past is their only inspiration in carrying on the struggle to preserve their national identity. Nowhere more than in Central and Eastern Europe is it true to say that modern development can only be understood in the light of medieval history.*

Francis Dvornik,
The Making of Central and Eastern Europe, 1949

STRÁŽNICE

Our first taste of Czecho-Slovakia was Králíky, a small highland town with a bumpy main square and delicious chocolate cake in the local café. A brightly lit vitrine displayed sugar-dusted pastries, and instantly we knew we were in the old territory of the Austro-Hungarians. We sat on a damp park bench in front of the shopping arcade and savoured our first cup of proper filter coffee with creamy fresh cake. Until now we had been drinking a poor imitation of Turkish coffee, a watery sludge with bits floating on top.

The car-park attendant came over to admire our bikes, and when I asked him about accommodation, he pointed out two places on the square:

'That one is long money and that one over there is short money,' he said in German.

He was a sweet old man with a friendly chuckle and I liked this country already. Another traveller arrived to sit on the neighbouring bench, a Czech hiker with canvas rucksack on his back. We acknowledged each other with smiles, and he took our example and fetched himself a pastry to eat. We sat together for a while, not speaking, but occasionally rolling our eyeballs skywards, as if to say, 'This rain!'

The weather did not let up until midday, and we flew towards the Moravian plain hardly being able to see the next hairpin bend. The descent was much steeper than our climb had been the other side, and for long stretches at a time we could simply cruise without effort. If only the road had not been so wet, we could have rocketed downhill. Nevertheless, we quickly came out of the dripping forests and joined a road tracing the young Morava, to be our guide until it joined the Danube at

Bratislava, near the Hungarian border. We could not see it yet, but we knew it was there.

A surge of adrenalin sent me racing ahead and I was as impatient as a child. This was the country with the most glittering capital of them all: Prague. This was a country that conjured up an atmosphere of *Sleeping Beauty* romance, yet also the hellish visions of Kafka, where helpless individuals become trapped in a spider's web of bureaucracy and unintelligible fate. Whatever we found here, it was bound to be memorable, though there was no reason for such optimism. I was letting myself get carried away by clichés and enjoying it too.

It was 60 kilometres before we stopped for the day, at a luxurious campsite outside the town of Mohelnice. The showers were steaming hot, and the soothing water felt wonderful on aching necks. Our muscles had cramped tight in the cold damp weather and we stood soaking for a very long time.

Later we set off for a sedate meal in the camp restaurant, where uniformed waiters served at tables covered in white tablecloths and a flower vase on each one. The menu was tailored to Germanic tastes, and we ate a delicious schnitzel with Morava beer. It was encouraging not to be the only foreign visitors for a change, and we even saw some other cyclists.

'Don't go to Czecho-Slovakia,' they had said in Poland.

'They've got a superiority complex. They want to out-German the Germans.'

But after less than twenty-four hours, we already felt more at home, more welcome and better fed than in Poland. The dour faces and depression had gone, replaced by unsought greetings and confident smiles. It was heartening, and though we were soon to discover that our popularity had much to do with our potential spending power, these positive feelings never wore off completely.

Next morning we woke up to blue skies with only faint streaks of cloud. We aimed to reach Olomouc, an easy 40 kilometres south-east, especially so because we had no option but to use a dual carriageway. Sudden gusts buffeted us every time a lorry passed by, but at least the road was flat and the rain gone, and we concentrated on getting ahead as fast as possible.

'Hi there,' came an American voice alongside us, and we found ourselves joined by three cyclists from the campsite. They slowed their pace for a chat and we compared routes and bicycles.

A woman and two men, they were students on an energetic tour of Europe. They were using mountain bikes with fat knobbly tires that must have made long distances hard work. Even so, the speed gradually increased, and Benoît and I both sweated to keep pace. 'I couldn't keep this up all day,' I hissed at Benoît, and he grimaced, as if to say even he would have problems. They released us soon enough, however, and the woman sped off, leading the way. We waved our farewells, and watched hot-faced as they switched into their cruising speed and disappeared over the horizon.

'Well, they're at least ten years younger than us,' I said, my pride dented. To be overtaken by men was one thing, but by another woman – my competitive nature was stung by that. At least I had the satisfaction of Benoît admitting to the same.

Olomouc, the former capital of Moravia, has a beautiful heart of baroque and renaissance architecture over a medieval design of irregular streets and cobbled squares. There is a distinctly Habsburgian atmosphere, especially around the ochre buildings of the Jesuit seminary and the university nearby and, except for the occasionally derelict backstreets and foreign language, you can easily imagine yourself in Austria. There is even a huge plague column on the main square, something I always associate with the Catholic south of German-speaking countries, who erected these monuments wherever people survived the dreaded Black Death.

All this comes as no surprise when you consider that the Habsburgs ruled over the Bohemian and Moravian territory from 1526 until the First World War. (Slovakia was ruled by the Hungarians from the ninth century onwards, which accounts for their distinct cultural heritage.) In fact, at the turn of the eighteenth century the combined effect of a brutal Counter-Reformation and the use of German as the official language meant that Czech had almost disappeared. The stifling bureaucracy of the Austro-Hungarian Empire virtually snuffed out the local cultures, which only revived once the foreign hold began to crumble, towards the end of the last century.

In the light of this, the Czech and Slovak nationalists' success in having a Czechoslovak Republic recognised in 1918 was an extraordinary achievement: a new country was born. More's the pity that it has now fallen victim to another nationalism, which has destroyed the Republic for the second time this century. (The first time was when the British and French governments sold out to Hitler in the Munich Diktat of 1938, sanctioning his occupation of the Sudeten region, where the majority of ethnic Germans lived.)

But we knew little of that when we were there in the summer of 1992, only soaking in the cultured atmosphere and wandering among the crowds on the main square. Classical music drifted from open windows above our heads, and posters announced poetry readings and many other events. The large student population ensured that this was a lively place, with not only high-minded events, but also rock music and open-air concerts.

The river Morava skirts around the old centre, and we strolled along its banks for the first time, past a gaudy Orthodox church with an odd pyramidal exterior painted salmon pink. A golden onion dome shone at the top, and with its successive layers of green copper roofs, the building looked more like a Christmas tree than a church.

Of course the town also had its share of post-war housing blocks and foul-smelling industry, and it was just our luck to find ourselves living next to the smelliest factory of all. The stench curled our nostrils: a mixture of burning plastic and rotten eggs. In fact, our accommodation was on the factory grounds itself, being the local truck stop for international deliveries. We found ourselves in a prefabricated block partitioned into single rooms, and I the only female in a place full of pot-bellied drivers waddling to the communal showers. I was grateful that the drunk in the middle of the night crashed into Benoît's room and not mine, and we were both glad to leave early the next morning. We had read about an outstanding art gallery in the town of Kroměříž, and intended to take time out to visit it on our way south.

By now the weather had recovered its summer climate, and we cycled on quiet country roads, past sunripe wheat and verges bobbing with wild flowers. There were no more poppies here, and I found that each country we passed through had a different flower lining our way. Rural Poland had been awash with the pillarbox red of its poppies, while here it was the delicate blue of cornflowers that caught the eye, soon to be joined by the shiny ripe fruit of black and red cherries. No more arcades of trees here, instead wide vistas over rolling countryside, with the mountains fading on the horizon behind us, the others coming into view to the east: the Beskydy mountains and White Carpathians.

Riverside Kroměříž followed the example of Olomouc, except that it was much smaller. A slanting main square glowed with freshly painted façades, and the main shopping street was alive with the fairground atmosphere of market day. A number of brand-spanking-new shops and cafés stood temptingly with their doors open, and we were easily drawn. Still dazzled by the rich food culture, we ordered chopped veal and mushrooms in a cream sauce, piled high on a bed of rice.

Once home to the bishops of Olomouc, the old palace is newly restored, and an elegant courtyard led through to the art gallery. The janitor looked down his nose at us, as if cycling pants and T-shirts were not suitable attire for appreciating art, and it was only my fluent German that managed to persuade him we could leave our bikes anywhere near the entrance. At last I was finding some use for it, and it remained an advantage from now on. Both Czecho-Slovakia and Hungary have a strong tradition of German-speaking tourism, as do the southern Balkans, where many Yugoslavs and Greeks have also spent time as 'guest workers' in Germany and speak excellent German.

Inside the gallery, two crones dropped their knitting to tear our tickets, and directed us to a rack of outsized slippers to cover our shoes. We shuffled like four-year-olds in our parents' slippers, conveniently polishing the parquet floor as we slid about. We had the rooms all to ourselves and it was tempting to behave as badly as the janitor's looks had implied. But the collection of sixteenth- and seventeenth-century painting was indeed impressive and demanded attention. There were some wonderful Bruegel paintings, so detailed in their portrayal of Flemish country folk: from the way they dressed to the tools they used. Cranach the Elder was also represented, his elegant figures eyeing you with cool diffidence.

Too soon it was time to get back to the energetic business of cycling, and now we regretted the heavy meal weighing down our stomachs. We regretted it even more shortly, when a mistake in Benoît's navigation sent us up over the Chřiby hills. It had looked like a shortcut on the map, but instead we found ourselves panting up a never-ending road, almost vertical at the base, and then torturing us with at least five steep ridges each of which always promised to be the last but never was.

We must have sweated for at least two hours, each small horizon of the road giving us hope, only to lead us on to a short ledge and a further hill looming beyond. If we had not been so exhausted we would have enjoyed the beautiful forest of beech and pine, clearings of glittering birch and young oak, and occasionally a lonely farm in a pool of sunshine. Instead we cursed the entire place and began to wonder if it would ever end. Both of us were reduced to pushing the bikes by now and grumbling insults. How could a few hundred metres of altitude be such hard work? But the cusp was around the same height as the border pass, and this time we had to get there without help from a train and a gentle approach.

At long last the forest opened up to reveal the Morava vale once more and we sighed with relief. Now we were rewarded with a rural idyll of cherry orchards and dozing villages tucked among steep pastures, and instantly our spirits revived. Juicy black cherries hung ripe for picking along the road, and soon our lips were burgundy with stolen fruit. In a tight valley below we could see the huge dome of a basilica, and a look at the map showed that we were above the Cistercian monastery of Veleh-rad and the nearest campsite too.

It was odd to find such a huge church here, but I read later that it was an important pilgrimage site, reputed to be where St Methodius lay buried, one of the most honoured saints for all Slavs. In fact, the Czechs were the first Slavs to be converted to Christianity by the missionary brothers Cyril and Methodius, in the late ninth century. They arrived from Greece in 863, and it was Cyril who invented the Cyrillic script, still used by the Orthodox East today, and in use by the Czechs for 200 years before Rome gained the upper hand and reintroduced Latin.

We raced past sleeping dogs too surprised even to bark, and the same distance just covered in two hours, we now made in thirty minutes. What bliss to sit unmoving on our bikes as we sped towards our goal. The sun was already casting long shadows by the time we reached the campsite, this time a simple affair tucked behind willow trees along a small stream.

We were greeted by a friendly middle-aged couple, who ran the site like an extension of their home. Roaming chickens came to inspect our tent, and two young children watched shyly from the wood-shed. The wife grilled us some delicious sausages, and when the husband saw how exhausted we were, brought cushions to soften the wood benches.

Benoît relished his first Urquell beer, according to him the best beer in the world, and even I liked it. A couple of those and we were ready for our sleeping-bags.

It was a beautiful site, but we could not help noticing the foul smell rising from the nearby stream, an ominous sign that all was not well in this apparent Eden. The industrial north of Bohemia and Moravia is notoriously poisonous, the entire country threatened by invisible death. Only Poland has higher percentages of drinking water deemed unfit for human consumption, and the pollution statistics here are just as frightening. The six major power stations of northern Bohemia alone produce almost twice as much sulphur dioxide as all of West Germany's put together, though they cater for a population barely 25 per cent the size.

It was extraordinary. For all our pleasure to be in Czecho-Slovakia, there was one aspect that had us completely flummoxed. In the short time we had been here so far we had eaten in restaurants six times, and four times we had been overcharged. The first time it happened we thought there must be some mistake: the bill simply did not add up to the total. But the waiter argued something about 'extra vegetables', and on second counting the bill came to yet another figure, which we paid rather than argue further. The next morning another waiter made the same 'mistake', and we vowed to check all menu prices against the bill from then on. This helped us once, when a soup had miraculously trebled in price when it came to paying.

'I'm new here,' she apologised.

After a few days we thought we had really got things under control by asking what the price of each item was before we ordered. But no. Even this was no protection, and we found ourselves arguing yet again:

'But she said a schnitzel was 45 koruna?'

'She knows nothing. The schnitzel is 39.50 koruna, plus chips is 9 koruna, plus salad is 10 koruna ...'

'Hang on, what salad?'

The waiter went off to get a sample of tinned beans that had formed a spoonful on our plates, and which we had not ordered. To us it had simply looked like decoration – a small relish.

'That's a salad?' I asked incredulously.

'You are in Czecho-Slovakia now,' growled the waiter, and I sensed that he had had this argument before. There was an air about him which said, 'If you don't like it why don't you go home?' Even we were rich compared to him, not to mention the majority of German-speaking tourists that annually came here. He bristled with resentment while I tried to reason with him, as if by refusing to be robbed peacefully I had insulted him.

So. Each item on our plates had a separate price, a variation we had not counted on, and a bill that should have been around 80 koruna in total came to 171 koruna instead. By the time this had been irrefutably established by the enraged waiter, Benoît was furious.

'If we weren't staying next door I'd walk out without paying. The fucker! Every time we get ripped off,' he exploded.

We could hardly believe it, but it really was happening almost every time we ate. My heart sank with the sight of each new menu, and it was beginning to spoil one of our favourite pastimes. What would be the trick this time? It seemed unfair to show mistrust right from the start, but by now we felt we really had to ask detailed questions before ordering anything.

First you had to establish whether prices were for the whole dish or just the meat. Then you had to check if the meat was priced by weight, in which case the size on your plate made a big difference. Then you had to watch out for anything you had not ordered and, finally, there was the matter of adding up the bill. But there was always some trick we had missed, and it was virtually impossible to get a fair deal.

It made you doubt your senses: on the one hand, people were polite, open and friendly, and on the other, we were constantly being cheated. What was strange to us was that this had never happened in Poland, a poorer country, where we had just as obviously been foreigners. Come to think of it, in all my travels I have never been relieved of my money so effectively, so often. I had to admire the ingenuity, and in the end we began to laugh about it. But I also had to think about the German lady I had met on the train, coming from Hamburg. Her prejudice against Poles had been firmly established by a single experience, and I dreaded to think how many more tourists returned from Czecho-Slovakia with stories like hers.

Of course anyone can harbour prejudices: an English boyfriend –
traumatised after visiting Dachau concentration camp – once told me that
no German had the right to self-respect, that the crime of the Nazis had
marked us all for ever and ever. I was stunned.

'What, even me?' I asked.

'Yes,' he said, with a finality that left me at once helpless and disgusted.

Apparently even educated, middle-class Labour voters could be rigid
prejudists if you scratched the surface, and in over a decade of living in
England I have found similar gut feelings come out again and again. A
time that stands out was during the Falklands War: smug feelings of
superiority, prejudice and, worst of all, unforgivingness and an insistence
on looking back instead of forward were common. There was a sense that
the British could set an example of humanity and democracy to others –
especially to 'continentals' or Argentinians – the crucial reference point
for all opinions not what could be, but what is because of the past. As
if it were impossible to develop new attitudes growing out of the potential of the present. And equally, as if it were an indestructible fact that the
British were, and always would be, an example of high civilisation to
others.

And how many arrogant Western visitors had it taken for Czech
waiters to lower themselves in this way? I had already seen enough
shameful behaviour in Berlin in 1989 to fear that the euphoria of East
meeting West would not last. I saw men come up to people in bars,
demanding to be bought a drink. 'You've had it good for forty-five years,
the least you can do is buy me a drink,' was the general line, and naturally
the response they got was rarely positive. Equally, people turning up in
their fat BMWs flaunting their material wealth did little to foster good
relations either.

Bars and restaurants are the most common place for differences in
culture and economics to be reduced to stupid contests, and everyone has
seen the ignorant tourist who complains about the local food or customs.
But in the present context of East and West Europe it is particularly
insidious. Our brothers and sisters have been reduced to our poor
relations all too soon, and the tendency to behave less than generously has
already spread on both sides of the old divide.

You do not have to be any great analyst to see that if European
governments do not take a positive lead, popular resentment on all sides

will only increase and nationalist and racist movements will gain an ever-growing number of supporters. The huge reservoir of moral courage that went into demanding a civilised society, the inspiration to believe in a better life is being allowed to wither, and the greatest opportunity for living up to the ideal of a democratic union of Europe is being squandered.

In fact, self-interest alone should dictate a massive aid operation, but instead Western banks stubbornly insist that the monstrous foreign debts of Hungary (around US$22.7 billion in 1992, or 72 per cent of GDP, according to the National Bank of Hungary) and others must be paid in full, giving them almost no chance at all to develop a market economy without excessive hardship and risking economic and political collapse. The lack of action also belies any Western pretensions to ecological concern, when there is such an obvious case for emergency assistance on their very doorsteps.

The world recession has made Western leaders short-sighted and inward-looking at the very moment they need to look ahead and beyond their borders. Instead they are prostitutes to power, and would rather turn to insular domestic issues than nurture future trading partners, ignoring the threat to peace that goes hand in hand with that stance. What a mockery of the European Community: at the same time border restrictions are supposed to be lifted between its members, the doors are being firmly slammed against those from the other side of the Economic Barrier.

The risk is great, however, since it is by no means guaranteed that East European countries will develop along peaceful democratic lines when most of them have no democratic tradition at all. Furthermore, the post-war generations have no experience of democracy whatsoever. If they are forced into severe privation an extreme response is almost inevitable under the circumstances, and the fledgling governments will fall.

Even as I write the news is full of violence against immigrants and refugees, mounting tensions between Hungary and Slovakia, reactionaries winning more votes in Poland and former Yugoslavia, street battles in Macedonia and killing in Bosnia. All this is grist to the mill of rabid nationalists, the military, and those of the old guard just waiting for a triumphant return, and already the struggling governments are resorting to ever more authoritarian measures to stay in control. No part of Europe will be able to keep the door locked indefinitely.

What a terrible irony that political freedom in Eastern Europe could well mean a quick return to power for the most repressive forces. Or, as Timothy Garton Ash put it: '1989 might then appear, to participants and historians, as just one brief shining moment between the sufferings of yesterday and those of tomorrow.'

These are not the things I had come to discover on this journey, yet they were proving inescapable. I was still looking for a positive response to the idea of our natural amity as Europeans, and I made a conscious effort to stay faithful to my original hopes. But it was becoming harder, and the idea of European unity was looking more fantastic all the time.

As luck would have it, we were just in time for the country's most important folk festival, which lay directly on our path. This, I thought, would be the perfect opportunity to see people at their best, and we set off for the small town of Strážnice in southern Moravia.

We arrived to find the party already under way. *Welcome*! cried a banner stretched above the main street: *Strážnice 92, 47th run of the International Folkloric Festival.* Underneath, loudspeakers fixed to street-lamps resounded with traditional music. The pavements were spilling over with ice-cream and hot-dog vendors, balloon and trinket sellers, and countless families milled about in excited anticipation. This afternoon the opening procession was going to take place, when all the visiting bands and dancing troupes would give us a twirl and a song on the main square. The mayor and his councillors were already getting microphones ready for the introductions, and we sped off to find the town campsite.

The site was next-door to the castle grounds where the festival was taking place, and a chaotic tent city spread out before us. People had come from all over, mostly young, and the atmosphere was a combination of holiday camp and pop festival. Bare-breasted youths lounged on the bonnets of their cars, radios blaring and a pile of empties gathering at their feet. Children played squeakily on a climbing frame, fathers dozed in their deckchairs, while mothers and sisters made sandwiches under the family parasol. For the first time on a campsite, we found ourselves not only surrounded by people, but local people. The jokes and laughter were carried on in Czech and Slovak dialects and we could understand nothing, only that we were welcome.

In the park of the castle grounds various stages had been erected on strategic clearings, and there were also three small stadiums for special performances. Groups of dancers and musicians were practising their routines in the shade of cyprus trees behind them, and the air was full of fiddle-playing and sonorous horns, whirling petticoats and clicking boots.

Many of the women's costumes reminded me of Bavarian dirndl dresses, with tight bodices over white blouses and crisp aprons over billowing skirts. The men wore knee-length trousers of green felt or leather, with finely embroidered waistcoats over Robin-Hood shirts. On their heads small hats sprouted boar's bristle or arching pheasant feathers, while the women wore neat headscarves. But there were plenty of variations on this theme, as well as others with a more Balkan character. One lady impressed me in particular, swaddled in layers of white linen tightly held in place by a red waistband and a beautifully embroidered apron. Her feet were tied into leather moccasins, and I imagined she must be from some remote Slovakian village, where Hungarians had ruled her people for centuries.

We ate lunch in the shade of the castle, where roast meats and sausages sizzled on open grills, and long wooden talbes creaked under the weight of huge beer barrels. Nearby a group of singing musicians was holding court to an enthusiastic audience. They were Moravians, and their male voices sang resonant and proud. We sat on the grass among the others, soon joined by two young men with their girls.

'Are you English?' one asked me, while his girlfriend hid her face. 'She wants to practise her English,' he laughed, and by the time our beers were finished we had swapped biographies, agreed the music was great, and compared cycling tips. The four of them planned to cycle to Greece themselves one day. But it was time for the main parade, and we tore ourselves away to join the throng. 'See you again some time.'

It seemed like every town and village had sent their best, and wave upon wave of Bohemians, Moravians and Slovakians danced and sang for us. There were even some foreign visitors, with a Bavarian oompah band, exotic Israeli women with lots of bare skin, as well as some rather graceless morris dancers. They humped their bodies around with audible effort, and it was obvious they had already imbibed rather too much of the local beer.

They were a poor example of English culture, and we could not help noticing that in spite of the endless supplies of cheap alcohol, no one was disgustingly drunk or behaving obnoxiously. Neither do I remember seeing a single policeman, which is extraordinary considering there were several thousand people here.

In the evening we mingled with the crowds once more, sampling a band here or dancing there, and finally a wonderful impromptu perform-ance of Moravian songs. We were back at the castle green, where the local bands played, and the fun began when a giant of a man set off a vocal duel with the performers. A beer bottle in one hand and cigarette in the other, his chest heaved as he released a magnificent tenor, his voice vibrating with operatic power. The crowd cheered him on and the band wisely invited him on to the stage.

Meanwhile couples came forward to dance on the makeshift wooden stage, and the floorboards creaked and bent under stamping feet. Young men in jeans and T-shirts were transformed: their heads held high and backs dead straight while their legs rose in balletic steps with pointed toes. What was impressive was that everyone seemed to know the dances and songs off by heart. These were not dusty folk-songs from a forgotten past, but a cherished part of their living culture.

Many of the songs were exclusively male, sometimes graceful and sad, other times fiercely energetic, and we were engulfed in a huge choir of voices, electrified by their fervour.

'This is the kind of thing wars are fought for,' said Benoît, and I could see what he meant. The tribal emotionalism was impressive but frighten-ing too. The argument that nothing is worth fighting for would find no welcome here. Rather, these were people who believed that some things are worth dying for. It was elemental, a passion borne of generations who have had to assert their identity by an act of faith while their lives were ruled by foreigners. This was the difference: what is nostalgic tradition in our culture, is nothing less than life blood here. It is a patriotism easily mistaken for nationalism, and unfortunately just as easily mobilised by unscrupulous leaders.

We came away from Strážnice with a heightened sense of what it meant to be proud of your culture – in the best spirit possible – and also with an inkling of the destructive energy that could be revived now the Russian winter is over.

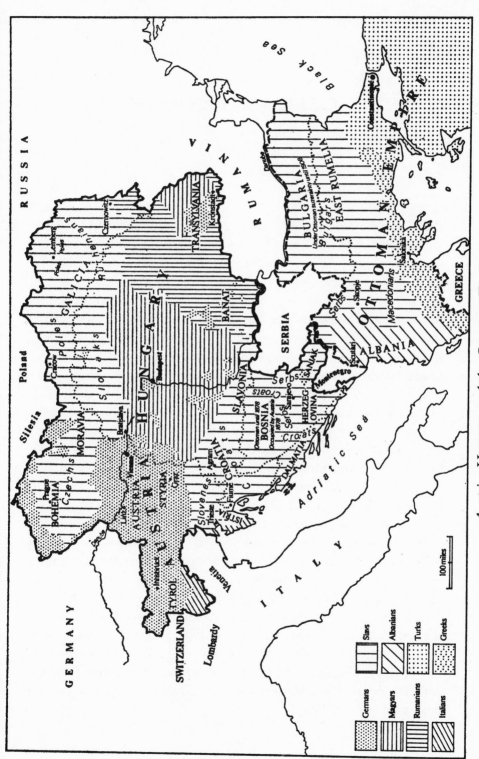

Austria–Hungary and the Ottoman Empire
From: *Europe Since 1870*, James Joll, Weidenfeld & Nicolson, 1973 (p. 170).

GERMANY

RUSSIA

Poland

Silesia

BOHEMIA

Czechs

MORAVIA

Slavs

GALICIA

Poles

Cracow

Lemberg

Czernowitz

Ruthenes

Slovaks

Bratislava

A U S T R I A – H U N G A R Y

Prague

Linz

SWITZERLAND

TYROL

Innsbruck

AUSTRIA

STYRIA

Graz

CARINTHIA

Slovenes

Trieste

Fiume

Agram

CROATIA

ISTRIA

Budapest

Danube

Vienna

B U K O V I N A

TRANSYLVANIA

Kronstadt

R U M A N I A

BANAT

SLAVONIA

Serbs

Croats

BOSNIA

HERZEGOVINA

Serbs

Sarajevo

Occupied Austria 1878

Ottoman until 1878

Croats

DALMATIA

Montenegro

SANJAK

SERBIA

Serbs

BULGARIA

Under Ottoman suzerainty until 1908

Bulgars

EAST RUMELIA

O T T O M A N   E M P I R E

Skoplje

Macedonians

ALBANIA

Scutari

Salonika

GREECE

Constantinople

Black Sea

Adriatic Sea

ITALY

Lombardy

Venetia

Germans

Magyars

Rumanians

Italians

Slavs

Albanians

Turks

Greeks

100 miles

CZECHO-SLOVAKIA

Bratislava, the Slovak capital, is an ancient city brutalised by modern architectural excesses. The most shocking sight is from the great castle that towers above the city. Throning a hill overlooking the Danube, the view must have been worthy of kings once: a vast horizon stretching beyond the Hungarian plain. Now your senses are insulted by fuming petro-chemical works and the hideous suburb of Petrzalka, connected to the city by a giant suspension bridge reminiscent of a two-pronged spaceship. Featureless housing blocks spread over a flat expanse of four square kilometres: box upon box in a huge nightmare of anonymity, where 160,000 people are crammed into their hutches, and it is no surprise to discover the estate has the highest suicide rate in the country.

Yet the city has a relaxed cosmopolitan air about it – a place you can easily spend some time, in spite of the ugliness, and we relished the big-city feel, even though it is actually no larger than Kraków. The ancient heart is undergoing a furious rehabilitation: scaffolding props up baroque façades and medieval walls. Street cafés have sprung up in all the choicest nooks and crannies. Courtyards have blossomed parasols and dainty tables, and street musicians play anything from classical to jazz. The offices of Aeroflot now share the scene with international fashion houses, and the local girls wiggle in the latest sexy dresses, even while headscarved country ladies waddle by with home-made bread and baskets of wine.

A delicious local delicacy is a deep-fried dough lashed with garlic and salt, called *langose*. It is served dripping with grease and full of carbo-hydrates, but wonderful all the same, and we looked forward to eating many more in Hungary, where the snack was said to originate. Food was definitely becoming a pleasure these days, and it was to improve the further south we travelled.

There was no shortage of places to mix with people well into the night, and we enjoyed ourselves among the different crowds. In the old quarter, street cafés were full of posturing students, and it was fun to watch them solving the world's problems in animated discussion or sitting with studied expressions of disinterest. They were sharp dressers too, and none of them would have looked out of place among the fashion slaves of London or New York.

In the beer halls and open-air shacks it was different. That was a male world of workmen, Gypsies and drunks: rowdier and less self-conscious, where waiters simply put glasses of beer before you unasked, replaced as soon as you were ready, and a biro notch on your beer mat for totting up the bill when you left.

We had reached the city in an easy two days from Strážnice, and were now at an important crossroads, where the Austrian and Hungarian lands meet the south-west corner of Slovakia. On the north bank is Slovakia, its western border traced by the confluence of the rivers Morava and Danube. On the south bank upriver is Austria, downriver is Hungary.

It is a place full of the historic confusions of the region: once known as Pozsony, when it was the Hungarian capital, it has also been Pressburg under the Habsburgs, and only Bratislava since 1918, when the new State was founded. The city has an invigorating atmosphere of a cultural melting pot, and significant numbers of Hungarians still live here. In fact, Hungarians make up a substantial ethnic minority in southern Slovakia, numbering over half a million people.

Vienna lies just 50 kilometres west, and pleasure boats cruise the Danube daily to that most sophisticated city. Others take the opposite direction to Budapest, and we toyed with the idea of floating into Hungary. The schedule announced four sailings daily, but, alas, we found a lack of customers had brought the service almost to a standstill. The next boat was not due for another two weeks and our plan had to be abandoned. It would have been fun to sail all the way to Budapest. But no matter – we had plenty to look forward to before reaching that city.

Bratislava was a good place from which to visit Carnuntum, the ancient ruins of an important Roman town, once the provincial capital of Upper Pannonia. It is situated close to the Danube, about 22 kilometres west, in what is now Austria, and used to be a major trading post for goods such as amber, brought to Roman merchants by the northern 'barbarians', who were lumped together under this phrase simply for being non-Roman.

Founded in about AD 10, Carnuntum was originally a garrison fortress, intended as a base for soldiers employed in the defence of the empire's north-eastern border, the *limes*. But the settlement quickly grew into a thriving town and, by AD 200, an estimated 1,200 inhabitants lived here alongside a regiment of 40,000 soldiers. In its heyday it had all the accoutrements of Roman comfort and ritual, from a centrally-heated bathhouse to a columned Diana temple, as well as magnificent villas built by the rich merchants.

This was the beginning of the *Via Ambra* (the Amber Road), which traced the most important trading route for amber at this time in history, and lead to the imperial homeland via the present Hungarian border towns of Sopron, Szombathely and Zalalövö; through modern Slovenia, via the towns of Ptuj, Celje, Ljubljana and Vrhnika; and finally to the Italian city of Trieste, known to the Romans as Aquileia, where expert craftsmen transformed raw amber into the luxury goods so fashionable among Roman ladies.

Even the bloodthirsty Emperor Nero was captivated by its charms, and we are told by Pliny that he ordered the manager of his gladiatorial exhibitions to buy as much as he could put his hands on. An equestrian soldier was duly sent to Carnuntum, from where he was to venture north, into the barbarian lands, to find out where exactly this mysterious substance originated.

He survived his adventure, and reported that amber was brought from 'about six hundred miles' beyond Carnuntum, from the northern coasts, and he returned to Rome with huge quantities of it, the largest piece believed to have weighed thirteen pounds.[1] The whole lot was used during one of Nero's gladiator shows, and it is said that the nets protecting the Emperor from the wild beasts shone magically with amber studs. Not only the nets either, but also 'the arms, the litters, and all the other apparatus, were decorated with nothing but amber.' Each day the

---

[1] Meanwhile the Roman historian, Tacitus, writing in the first century, tells us that amber comes from the coastal lands of the Aestii, who he believed were the only Germanic tribe to 'ransack the sea' for amber. Rather condescendingly he writes in his *Germania*: 'Like true barbarians, they have never asked or discovered what it is or how it is produced ... They gather it crude, pass it on in unworked lumps, and are astounded at the price it fetches.'

designs were varied, the use of amber in this way an outrageous ostenta-
tion at the time.

The Golden Age of amber trading did not last long, however, for by
the year AD 375, a traveller described Carnuntum as a 'dirty, abandoned
nest', which had been destroyed by invading barbarians from the East the
year previously. And so it remained for around seven hundred years – the
earliest evidence for subsequent habitation only dating from the year
1100, when the ancestors of present-day Petronell arrived – an insignificant village ignored by the motorway from Bratislava to Vienna.

I decided to hitch-hike there since I had no wish to cycle on such a fast
road, and positioned myself at the beginning of the motorway. It was only
a short distance, but I was not entirely comfortable about going alone,
especially since there was a border to cross. But there was no other way to
get there, and Benoît's visa was only for a single entry into Czecho-
Slovakia. It made no sense to lose it for one day outside the country,
especially when we had no idea if the ruins were worth seeing. But I was
not given much time to hesitate and was in luck almost immediately,
picked up by a self-satisfied Mercedes driver.

'I have everything a man could want,' he told me.

He was a businessman from Vienna, with a special commercial passport
that gave him unfettered access to all the East European countries. He
made regular trips to the capitals beyond the old Iron Curtain, but he had
not learnt to like any of them yet, least of all the people.

'They are all scoundrels or work-shy,' he informed me.

I told him a little about my journey, and when he heard we were
staying in a workers' pension in Bratislava he was horrified.

'It must be disgusting?' he asked rhetorically, and went on to say he
never stayed anywhere other than the top hotels. 'At my age I only have
time for luxuries.

'I take what pleases me', he breezed, and twice let his hands brush my
knees. I told him about my Canadian husband waiting in Bratislava, and
he launched into a story about diving in the Caribbean with friends from
Montréal. I was appalled by this man's smug attitude of superiority, and
glad the journey only took twenty minutes in his fast car. At least he left
the motorway to drop me off at the ruins themselves, and let me go
without hesitation.

I shared the ruins with a hoard of schoolchildren, proudly shown around by the local guide, who reminded them that Carnuntum is the only museum exclusively dedicated to the country's Roman legacy. In fact, there was not much to see except the foundations of the living quarters and bathhouse. The temple was being rebuilt and was out of bounds, so we had to make do with an artist's impression and I could see the kids' attention fading.

The Austrian authorities are doing their best to restore the most striking features of Carnuntum, such as the temple and the amphitheatre. But for the moment the site is hardly impressive, and I was glad not to have pressured Benoît into coming with me. To have made him get a new visa for a pile of old stones would have been pushing his tolerance a bit too far. He has no cultural chip on his shoulder, which is one of the things I like about him, and antiquity alone elicits no response. He thinks nothing of discarding monuments that have only their history to offer, but I was glad to have come all the same. This was one of the rare tangible links in my search for the amber trade routes.

I walked back up to the motorway and soon I was heading east again, this time in a small Fiat, sitting next to a friendly Slovak chemist. He lived in the dreaded Petrzalka housing estate, and told me that to add insult to injury the government was now trying to offload the apartments on to the inhabitants, attempting to persuade them to buy their council flats so the authorities could save on maintenance costs. Even if they had wanted to, he explained, nobody had the money to do so. They had had to pay large bribes to get housed at all, and most people were still paying off those debts. It was going to take a long time too, since the average wage of US$200 per month was no better than in Poland.

It was a strange feeling stepping into the old West for just one day. I felt like I had briefly jumped ship, but was glad to be returning back to the land where they say *ahoj* for 'goodbye'. The perfection and efficiency of the Austrian villages was somehow unattractive, lacking in something which I can only call generosity of spirit.

I was surprised to feel like this, especially since I had had plenty of opportunity to see and experience the downside of Poland and Czecho-Slovakia. Perhaps I was simply reacting against individuals: the Mercedes driver and the 'rules are rules' ticket man at Carnuntum, who had refused to accept Czech crowns. Yet I was relieved to pass through the border without much let, and my friend the chemist agreed, still amazed at how easy it was when he had been used to living in the shadow of watch-towers for so long.

I asked him about the possible split of his country. Already all official literature in Bratislava used a hyphen in the word Czechoslovakia, which we had thought rather spurious. But he seemed to think the split was inevitable, though he was equally convinced it would take place without violence.

'The Czechs and Slovaks have no tradition of spilling blood between them,' he argued, 'but this separation should have happened a long time ago. For a thousand years the Hungarians ruled our land and kept us as serfs. Then we were dominated by the Czechs, ruled from Prague without any regard for our interests. They have never listened to us. They suppressed our language and always gave political power to their own kind.'

He was talking about the centralised control from Prague, and said even Václav Havel had made himself unpopular.

'When he was elected he talked just like a typically arrogant Czech, with no appreciation of our problems.'

These were harsh words for a man apparently so popular – especially in the West – but it betrayed the deep resentment many Slovaks feel about having been kept in rural servitude for so long, sharing little of the wealth created by the industrial revolution that took place on Moravian and Bohemian soil.

Slovakia had to assert its independence for its people's own interests, for their very cultural survival, he explained. Otherwise their standard of living, their traditions and language would never flourish. I asked how he thought his new country would survive economically if it was so poor, and he responded that the huge community of Slovaks in America would surely send the necessary aid. (Twenty per cent of the Slovak population emigrated in the late nineteenth century and early years of this century, almost all to the USA.) Wishful thinking, I thought to myself, but came away with a better idea of just how deep the divisions between Czechs and Slovaks are.

Nothing less than national identity is at stake, and once again it was only possible to understand the depth of feeling by finding out the history behind it. Slovaks have been dreaming about independence for centuries. They are a people who have almost never had a country to call their own, and nothing will stop them now their chance has come. So far their only ally has been the Catholic Church, which is yet another aspect of their fundamental differences with Czechs, the majority of whom are not particularly religious. By contrast Slovaks tend to be deeply religious and conservative, with little sympathy for the new 'liberal' politics in Prague.

It was time for us to experience Prague for ourselves, and once more we put our bikes into storage before catching a train for the erstwhile capital of Czecho-Slovakia. It was our second major detour, and the treat we had been waiting for.

Prague is the Paris of Eastern Europe, eliciting the same kind of excitement born of romantic fantasies and a vibrant cultural life. Astride the Vltava River, the setting is magnificent: grand stone bridges connect the steep ascent to the royal mount with the ancient city across the water. Peaceful riverside walks contrast with the hurly-burly tourist trail up to the castle; while in the city centre there is a mixture of spacious avenues and hidden squares, where baroque palaces mix easily with early twentieth-century buildings, busy shopping streets with elegant cafés and proud hotels.

Prague has never suffered much damage by human hand or natural disaster, and the city oozes history from every brick. Medieval alleyways and squat artisan cottages cluster under the great castle and the mansions of illustrious merchants. Smooth pastel surfaces from the seventeenth and eighteenth centuries give way to blackened apartment blocks with wrought-iron balconies, and only Vienna can rival the rich heritage of perfectly preserved art nouveau architecture, complete with original interiors.

It was these *Jugendstil* buildings that thrilled me most, ranging from the elaborate mosaics decorating the Prague Insurance Building on Narodni Street, to the faded elegance of the Hotel Europa on Wenceslas Square and, most of all, the glorious *Obecní dům*, the concert hall built just after the turn of the century. Its café and restaurant are still in pristine style, the best details in the lighting, ranging from exuberant droplet bulbs hanging from high ceilings, to more linear, almost art deco shapes for the table lamps. There are even some original paintings by Alphonse Mucha, one of the finest artists of the age, whose work has travelled the world on countless postcards.

We found a 'cheap' student hostel to stay in, situated high above the city beyond the castle, and spent our evenings wandering around the cobbled streets of Prague's left bank. This was the romantic, fairy-tale quarter, clinging to the slope beneath the royal fortress and opening on to Charles Bridge, the quintessential image of the city, punctuated by photogenic statues and voluptuous lampposts.

Trinket vendors, T-shirt and postcard sellers, portrait sketchers, hippy hair-plaiters and musicians lined the bridge, and a steady flow of tourists moved like lava down the hill and across the river. One evening a couple of singers even brought their own piano, and dressed in black coat tails they stole the show, their classical songs the perfect music for this setting.

Around the markets of the Staré Město, the heart of the city on the right bank, lively commerce carries on under fading apricot walls, and it is hard to imagine that only a few years ago these same people had to queue for basic necessities each day. The smell of fruit and vegetables from all over the world mixes with the sizzling chips and sausages at hot-dog stands; while in the evenings, the surrounding wine bars turn the pavements busy with office workers and students.

At the market one day, a wizened old lady passed hunched over her shopping and but for a small image I would have hardly noticed her: the sleeves of her dress only reached to her elbows, and I caught a fleeting glimpse of a tattooed number on her skinny forearm. She must have been a young girl when they came to get her, and my imagination strained to comprehend her fate. It was a reminder that Prague has seen many human catastrophes, even if its buildings have remained unspoilt. Josefov, formerly the Jewish quarter, makes up the northern part of the Staré Město, and the lopsided gravestones in the old cemetery there are one of the most haunting sights of the city.

We had been travelling for a month by now, and decided to celebrate in a cosy restaurant away from the crowds. We had come a long way since crossing the border to Swinoujście, and Poland already seemed in the distant past. Our journey had taken on a different character in the exuberant atmosphere of this more colourful country and, without a serious language problem, much of the anxiety had disappeared. Most of all, I was pleased and relieved to discover I enjoyed travelling with Benoît.

As I said before, the idea of travelling with someone – let alone a husband – had always been out of the question. I had tried it once, and it had been a total failure. I was eight years old, and for some trifling reason I decided to run away with my best friend Jennifer. We were living in Canberra/Australia at the time, so running away meant heading into the Australian bush.

I persuaded Jennifer to stay at my house and, equipped with an apple and some biscuits, we climbed out of the bedroom window early one morning. Living in the suburbs, we soon reached wild scrubland, and I was really enjoying myself when Jennifer began to cry. She was already feeling guilty, and when a snake reared up nearby, she completely lost her nerve and we had to beat a humiliating retreat to my poor parents. I vowed from then on never to travel in company again.

Yet now, twenty-two years later, I was not only with someone else, but with a man, the kind I had always thought could not possibly exist: one with the freedom of spirit to come halfway around the world with me, unthreatened by my dreams and obsessions, but not disrespectful of them either. A traveller, yet, unlike me, without a specific driving ambition, and without a career that rooted him to one spot. In other words: a soul mate. Still I had hesitated at the prospect of doing this journey together. The risk had seemed great.

Weighed against my doubts, however, had been the experience of living together, which had shown me that even if I was not easy to get on with, Benoît certainly was. There had been no reason to doubt he would keep this trait while travelling, and now my reluctant faith was being rewarded. There had been bad moments, but always caused by specific practical problems. Like the time Benoît destroyed the balance of our back wheels by over-enthusiastically adjusting the spokes; or the time I lost expensive tickets to see one of the shows during the Strážnice festival. In either case we had let each other off the hook and managed not to stew for too long.

One of the most interesting evenings we spent in Prague was in a local beer hall, sitting at long tables with a hundred voices echoing from the vaulted ceiling. We got talking to a carpenter drinking opposite us.

'You speak English?' he asked. 'I learn English just with a book and cassettes, but I like to practise.'

He was friendly and constantly bursting into a single, explosive laugh.

'Ha!' he would shout, while we talked about languages. 'Dutch is catastroph!'

'What about Slovak?'

'Ha! Catastroph!'

It was a raucous evening, and we laughed at our poor linguistic talents. Naturally we also spoke of the imminent split between Czechs and Slovaks, and he explained that part of the problem, as he saw it, was that Slovaks have no cultural tradition compared to the Czechs. The ancient Czech culture and proud national history stands apart, and Czechs find the countrified Slovaks rather vulgar and loud, with primitive passions that can be dangerous. After all, look what happened when they had a chance to run their own affairs: with the connivance of the Catholic Church, a Nazi puppet state of Slovakia was declared in 1939, lasting until the end of the Second World War. Our friend hastened to add that he did not necessarily agree with the snobbish prejudice between Czechs and Slovaks, but there it was nevertheless.

Our last night in Prague we met a much less endearing fellow. He was a Finn, who had adopted the city as a second home and was keen to show his expertise.

'The food looks good,' I said, to make conversation while we waited for our supper.

'Well, that's because you're British,' he condescended. 'Britain has the worst food in the world,' he said, pronouncing the common view.

Benoît and I let the conversation die after this, ate our food, and left. But, all in all, our time in Prague was as magical as we had hoped it would be, and I was very glad to have seen the city before it becomes too sanitised and enslaved to tourism. The tarting up has carried on apace since 1989, and I found it almost too much already: everything was a bit too clean and perfect, a bit too cute, and the prices were astronomical compared to the rest of the country.

The shiny new McDonald's charged the same for a Big Mac and chips as you could pay for a full meal with wine outside the capital. The busy open-air tables served beers at seven times the usual price, and accommodation at every level was priced on a par with the West.

Of all the European cities, only Venice can rival Prague for her enchanting beauty, yet there is no month left in the calendar when you can visit the canals without rubbing shoulders with countless others. Now it is Prague's turn to sell herself, her lovers pushed aside for paying customers. Anyone can have her, and we were two of them.

Back in Bratislava we decided to visit the Slav counterpart to Carnuntum: Devín Castle, which guards the confluence of the Morava and Danube, about 10 kilometres north-west of the city. A riverside road leads swiftly there, past small vineyards and kitchen gardens, and weeping willows trailing branches in the Danube.

We arrived to find a small fair under way beneath the castle mound, an unexpected and welcome surprise that made our visit doubly worthwhile. Devín, which means 'young girl' in old Slovak, is an important symbol of Slav heritage, and the regional nationalists have not failed to use it in their propaganda. They have been coming here for inspiration ever since self-determination became an issue in the nineteenth century and, even while we were there, a cavalcade of black BMWs arrived to fire up the crowd with political speeches. The air was full of megaphone voices, shrieking infants and rousing songs from the revellers drinking beer at long wooden tables. Small troupes of fiddle and accordion players moved among them, and their joyful tunes mixed chaotically with the neighbouring tinkle of merry-go-rounds and pop songs blasting from hot-dog stands.

Meanwhile the empty sockets of Devín's ruined fortifications gazed from on high, perched on a natural promontory of rock and limestone just over 200 metres above the joining rivers. The grey waters of the Morava moved sluggishly into the swift current of the Danube, and the two rivers embraced in swirling whirlpools. It was a fine view from up here, where you could see for miles and miles into the southern plain of Austria and Hungary, as well as anyone approaching on the waterways, and it was easy to see why a castle had been built on this ideal spot. Not only had it been an important border post between ancient territories, but also a vital staging post on the historic amber trade routes. The earliest of these lead south to the Aegean, which was our chosen path, while the Roman trade would have headed upriver, to the *Via Ambra* beginning at Carnuntum.

The site has been occupied for thousands of years, though very little evidence remains to be seen today. Only crumbling walls and a few lonely keeps stand now, the rest destroyed by Napoleonic soldiers in 1809. But the view alone is worth the visit, enhanced for us by the storks, who have built their summer nests among the broken ledges.

Our return to the city coincided with the end of the fair, and the buses were crammed to breaking point. The crowd squeezed into the seats and aisles, packing bodies so tight that children were wedged between bony knees and we stood pressed to unfamiliar bosoms. A fight broke out at the door, and an old man was unceremoniously pushed off by a determined grandmother. She shoved him so hard that he almost fell, but she clung defiantly to her space and the doors snapped shut behind her.

It was an extraordinary display for an old woman, and brought back memories of Munich grandmothers, always pushing and shoving and demanding your seat without so much as a thank you in return. The ones on the Prague trams were just the same, and Benoît had found himself at the sharp end of a walking stick more than once. Perhaps it is their revenge for neglect at home. Certainly as a child I remember looking forward to when I could be that obnoxious and get away with it.

After a week of sightseeing and city life it was a relief to get back to the peaceful solitude of cycling, and we set off the next day. We had enjoyed ourselves in Czecho-Slovakia, and both agreed that we would happily return some day, especially to the Moravian hills and Bratislava. But, for now, our journey was taking us to Hungary, and we crossed the riverine border at Komárno, following the Danube's path on the Hungarian side from then on. We would see two more capitals along its banks if all went well: first Budapest, and then Belgrade, almost 400 kilometres further downriver.

3. HUNGARY

By twisting the arms of East European governments and insisting that aid will be linked with quite specific economic developments, the West is making a fundamental contribution to instability in Eastern Europe that is in nobody's interests; indeed, it is stimulating anti-Western and anti-capitalist popular sentiment.

Misha Glenny,
The Rebirth of History, 1993

AROUND THE BEND

Komárno was Komárom on the Hungarian side, which was one of the few names that seemed remotely pronounceable that day. How on earth did you say Nyergesújfalu or Pilisszentkereszt? There were some longer words than that too, but I cannot remember them.

The Hungarian language is unlike any other in the region, with almost no Latin or Slav roots that one could recognise, and all we could do was marvel at the strange-looking words, sprinkled liberally with accents and umlauts alike. Hungarian belongs to the Finno-Ugric linguistic group, which is to say it is a development of the original language spoken by the early south-west Asians (Caucasians), who first populated what is today Finland and Hungry. There are remote similarities between modern Finnish and Hungarian, but not sufficient for mutual understanding, especially not since Hungarian has also been shaped by Turkish, Russian and German. In fact, modern Hungarian has most in common with the language spoken by people living on the eastern reaches of the Ural mountains.

We had little hope of even learning the basics in the short time we would be in the country, but at least I could communicate in German, and nobody seemed to mind. There was just one word I instantly recognised when I saw it, and that was *kolbász*, for 'sausage'. What had been *kiełbasa* in Poland was *klobásy* in Czecho-Slovakia, and would be *kobasice* in Serbia.

The majority of Hungary's people are Magyars, descendants of a group of nomadic tribes that came from the steppes west of the Russian river Don, and conquered this region towards the end of the ninth century. They were renowned horsemen and notoriously vicious fighters, which is why they often get mixed up with the Huns, who actually belong to a much earlier age, and did not survive past the fifth century. The word 'Hungary' is believed by some to be a misnomer first used by West Europeans, who mistook the Magyar 'hordes' for Huns. In fact, the name results from the original Bulgar-Turkish word *Onogur*, in use in the seventh century, which literally means 'the ten arrows', and refers to the federation of ten tribes that eventually came to be dominated, ethnically and linguistically, by the Magyars. (The German word for Hungary is *Ungarn*, in French it is *Hongrie*.)

In contrast to the Huns the Magyars have survived very well, and it was they who destroyed the earliest Slav empire, the Great Moravian Empire, in 906, and put a wedge between the northern Slavs of Poland, and the southern Slavs of former Yugoslavia. In spite of the devastating Mongol invasions in the thirteenth century, Turkish conquest in the sixteenth century, and almost two centuries of Austrian rule, the Magyar people, their culture and language have never been obliterated. This is truly amazing if you consider that the mass exterminations and destruction wrought by the Mongols destroyed between 50 per cent and 80 per cent of all settlements and reduced the population by up to 30 per cent in some regions. It was devastation on a scale unparalleled in Europe at the time, only to be repeated with greater effect three centuries later, when 150 years of Turkish occupation decimated the population by up to 50 per cent in areas such as Transylvania and on the plain, between the Danube and the Tisza rivers. It did not recover until early this century – repeated epidemics of plague and smallpox slowing up the demographic curve considerably.

No wonder their history of survival is a source of great pride to Hungarians, and they guard their heritage as jealously as anyone else in this part of the world, the more so for being surrounded by 'alien' people. No doubt for this reason it also still rankles badly that the Allies forced them to concede the former territories of southern Slovakia and Romanian Transylvania (to Hungarians – Felvidék and Erdély respectively) after the First World War – not to mention the Serbian province of Vojvodina, also formerly Hungarian – which altogether resulted in the loss of over three million people to the nation and reduced the country's size by more than a third. According to the historian P. F. Sugar, the loss was even greater. Excluding the Croatian territory, he states that Hungary lost 67 per cent of her land and 58 per cent of her population. Whatever the exact figures, the humiliation was severe and is not forgotten in the slightest.

All this was the result of the treaty of Trianon, reluctantly signed by Hungary at Versailles in 1920, because she was on the losing side of the First World War. There had been no choice, since her ties to the Austro-Hungarian Empire, which was forcibly allied to the German cause, decided the matter out of hand. Now this treaty, which is considered totally unjust by all Hungarians, is one of the sources of potentially violent conflict as once more the region's countries jostle for position in the new order of Europe. Deep-seated resentments are resurfacing that it will be very hard to resist acting upon.

The road we were on followed the Danube exactly, and we cycled within sight of its mighty waters flowing east. Soon, however, the Börzsöny and Pilis highlands were going to force the river into changing course, turning it due south into the Carpathian basin and the city of Budapest. Already the river was gathering speed as it was being squeezed tighter, and even motorised boats had to strain hard to stay on course. Our first stop was Esztergom, unusually easy to pronounce and the most significant town along what is known in tourist brochures as the 'Danube Bend'.

We found a campsite down by the riverbank with a hand-painted sign announcing *We are happy to welcome our first guests this year*, and inside a further sign asked for understanding as the hosts were still learning their trade. It was a small place that had cheekily opened almost next-door to a very fancy campsite with everything from restaurant to private swimming-pool. Most visitors clearly still preferred the Western comforts laid on in the established campsite, but we were happy to support the smaller outfit, and did not mind the primitive showers, especially not when we were paying around US$3 in all, which was a third of the other's rate.

It was a balmy evening, and we decided to stay by the riverside instead of exploring the town. An open-air restaurant nearby enticed us to its tables, and soon we were eating our first Hungarian meal, drinking crisp white wine from the local vineyards, and watching the sun go down over the willow trees. Once more there were familiar Austro-Hungarian dishes, like schnitzel and goulash, but also specifically indigenous meals, like chicken in paprika sauce or *töltött-kaposzta*, which is cabbage stuffed with meat and rice, and *töltött-paprika*, green peppers stuffed with meat and rice in a tomato sauce.

We sat with a Danish pensioner, who told us he had been coming here in his camper van for fifteen years: that is how much he enjoyed the local food and culture, not to mention the cheap prices. For us, on our limited budget, prices had been getting progressively more expensive, but at least the value for money also seemed to be increasing.

To the consternation of the waiter we scrutinised our bill in detail – as was our habit since Czecho-Slovakia – but he soon relaxed when we explained our reasons.

'Czecho-Slovaks very bad!' he said, jabbing his thumb down.

'What about Yugoslavs?'

'Yugoslavs very bad!'

'Austrians?'

'Very bad!'

'Romanians?'

'Very bad!' he shrugged, all of them getting a decisive thumbs down. It struck us as a little paranoid at the time, but his attitude was to prove representative of a common gut feeling in Hungary.

In the morning we walked into Esztergom, past the rust-stained stumps of a bridge that once connected with Slovakia, on the other side of the river. The travel writer Patrick Leigh Fermor crossed it almost sixty years ago, transfixed by the sight of peasants and grandees making their way up to the country's most famous basilica above the town. When he was here, the ordinary people still wore traditional dress, with the women in finely embroidered bodices and coloured ribbons in their hair, and their masters in magnificent furs and with jewel-encrusted scabbards for their swords. But history has swept away such sights for ever, just like the bridge itself, which was blown up by the retreating Germans in 1945.

We could still visit the basilica, though, and we climbed the short path to its hilltop platform. It was here that Stephen, one of the Magyars' earliest rulers, was crowned the country's first Christian king, later to become their patron saint after his death in 1038. Inside the cathedral, cold marble made for an austere nave, and our voices echoed from the huge cavern of a dome, 100 metres high at the crown. The nineteenth-century interior was strangely at odds with the antiquity of this sacred place, but the original church was destroyed by the conquering Turks, and the present building was only begun in the last century. The effects of history seemed inescapable at every turn on this journey, a fact I was soon to be confronted with more forcefully.

We ate our first Hungarian *lángos*, which were identical to the ones we had found in Bratislava, only here you could choose from a whole range of toppings, our favourites being garlic sauce or grated cheese, and delicious honey in the mornings. Each one the size of a dinner plate, they could easily keep you going for hours.

We set off into the Bend, and found ourselves cycling alongside picturesque hills covered by forests and the neat contours of vineyards. Grey rocks jutted out to form ideal perches for medieval castles and, sure enough, we shortly passed underneath the ruins of Visegrád castle, towering at least a hundred metres above the river. The landscape reminded me of the romantic paintings of German and Italian art and, but for the modern traffic and holiday homes by the water, the scene fitted exactly.

Now the Danube no longer marked the border between Hungary and Slovakia, the Börzsöny hills pushing the line further north while the river turned south, to run straight through the heart of Hungary. A large island appeared, and we decided to cross over to it, a gentle breeze keeping us cool while we cycled past acres of nodding sunflowers. This was the flower for Hungary: a spray of yellow petals around a shiny face of seeds, each one standing man-high on a sturdy trunk. Later, on the Hungarian plain, sunflower fields often stretched as far as the eye could see, and I enjoyed them just as much as the poppies of Poland.

It was time to return to the mainland by the last ferry crossing, and we rolled on to an iron barge running between the island and the west bank on a steel cable. The ticket man charged us for two tickets each, one for every person and bike. Yet I noticed that another passenger only payed half our price, and he was in a car. So much for the much-prized integrity! A woman with baskets of freshly picked apricots tried to sell us a few kilos of her harvest, and I wished we had more room in our panniers. I bought a handful instead, but she looked disappointed.

The island is called Szentendrei and tapers off almost exactly opposite the ancient little town of Szentendre, the last of the Danube Bend resorts before the suburbs of Budapest. The place is a popular tourist spot because of its picture-book setting and cobbled streets. It was discovered by artists at the turn of the century, and the narrow lanes and alleys are crammed with art galleries and trinket shops, expensive restaurants and wine bars, where tourists mingle with the *noveau riche* from Budapest. It's a kind of St Tropez of the Danube and, although the restored fishermen's houses are very pretty, the place is more artificial than arty, and we did not like it much. This time there was no escaping the posh campsite, but at least we enjoyed the attendant swimming-pool in the last hours of daylight.

The only place to find an ordinary supper was the train station, and we stood amongst the drunks and locals, drinking good wine from plastic cups and eating grilled sausages and mustard. On our return to the triangular central square we found a visiting operatic company about to perform *The Barber of Seville* and the false air of sophistication was complete. Now the crowd with video cameras was replaced by dressed-up spectators ready for some 'high culture', and we enjoyed ourselves sneaking in amongst them without paying. What snobs we all were!

Our Danish friend from Esztergom had kindly told us about his favourite campsite for Budapest, which was small and friendly, and had a regular bus connection into the city. It sounded like just the place for us, and we set off for Üröm, a village on the northern edge of the capital. Judging by our map we thought we would be there in no time: it was only 12 kilometres. But we soon found ourselves struggling up and over a vine-clad ridge, west of the river, and it was a very sweaty couple that arrived to meet Juliusz, the proprietor.

His site was indeed small, no more than one acre; shading willow trees lining the edge of an immaculate lawn, and a neat gravel path marking an inner circle for caravans. There were hot showers and even washing-machines and, best of all, free use of a kitchen and fridge. This was no ordinary campsite but the highly personalised domain of its owner, who did his utmost to make all his guests feel welcome. He had been the manager once, but now this was his private property and he was doing very well. It was the ideal base from which to explore Budapest: a peaceful country home right next to the big city.

We took the next bus into Budapest and quickly found ourselves in the largest city we had seen so far. Two million people live here, which represents 20 per cent of Hungary's entire population, and dodging the crowds and busy traffic we really felt it. The pace here was as hectic as in London and I felt a little intimidated, especially since the unfamiliar signs and language made orientation that much more difficult. But we found our way to the centre without too much trouble, and I had the address of Hungarian PEN, where I hoped to make contact with a few writers, preferably young ones, that might share my excitement about the future of a united Europe and the first chance to mix freely.

As luck would have it, the PEN office was bang in the middle of the city, on Vörösmarty ter, the most elegant square of the neo-classical Pest district, where the famous *Pâtisserie Gerbeaud* recalls a glamorous past, when this was the Habsburg Empire's second capital. The café society that once met here has long gone, of course, but the atmosphere around the square is as sophisticated as ever, and we both noticed the flair of the city's women. They seemed to have embraced modern chic with complete confidence, and Benoît enjoyed their freely bouncing breasts. No Catholic modesty cramped their style and according to Benoît it was not just the food that was getting better. There are many attractive women in Budapest and the sex industry is booming – one of the less salubrious benefits of democratic freedom.

Imre Szász, the general secretary of Hungarian PEN, was not in the day I called. But I made an appointment to see him the following morning, and he generously gave me an hour of his time. He had the air of an immensely tired person about him, someone exhausted by fate, and he sat in a darkened office, as if excessive light might be unbearable. His voice was gravelly from chain-smoking.

'What can I do for you?' he asked with a professional air, and I self-consciously tried to explain why I was here. I was uncomfortably aware of how irrelevant my project might appear to him – after all, travel writing hardly counts as 'literature' – and I felt a bit like an imposter. I had co-authored two books and written two myself, yet still I felt I should not count myself a real writer, not like novelists and poets. Then again, I have heard of authors with a string of books to their name who still do not have the confidence to call themselves a writer, so perhaps there was no need for me to feel paranoid.

At any rate, Mr Szász gave me his full attention and willingly gave me some telephone numbers. He agreed that it would be best to speak to younger people, nearer my own age, who would be less damaged by the past and more hopeful for the future. His generation was too full of bitterness for their prime lost under communism, especially their writing prime. So much energy was lost in just surviving with integrity, many, like him, having paid the price of persecution and imprisonment.

I got the impression that for Mr Szász the joy of Hungary's new freedom was tempered by the fact that it could well be too late for him to benefit. In spite of the new era, it will be a long time before there is money for a vibrant publishing economy, and in the meantime the world recession makes a wider audience through translation even more unlikely than before.

As for the improved living standards; 'I'd prefer more telephones and less pornography,' he said, voicing one of the most common complaints in the city. It is expected to take years before a new telecommunications network can be installed and, until then, private householders as well as businesses can but dream of their own telephone, not to mention the existing ones working properly. The whole system is hopelessly inefficient and as long as Hungary struggles with its US$22.7 billion foreign debt the pace of change will be excruciatingly slow.

'The city spends precious time and money on superficial changes, like renaming all the streets whose names glorify communism. But all that is window-dressing, and the real needs are not being addressed.'

For us the new names were doubly confusing, since none of the maps had been reprinted. There was no way of knowing the new name until one actually found the relevant street, where the signs themselves showed the old name crossed out in red and the new name above it. Depending on the age of the passers-by we asked, they would either remember the pre-war name of a street or square, or simply shrug their shoulders, as confused as we were.

Visiting a bank we found more evidence that Hungary's new status is strictly limited: it was possible to change as many US dollars into Hungarian forints as you liked. But it was impossible to find a bank that would convert forints back into dollars. It had been the same in the other countries we had cycled through, who not only refused to buy back their own currency but also refused to accept their neighbour's money, and we had to take care not to get stuck with worthless currency.

Perhaps the only level on which the concept of a united Europe can survive is on the economic and political level, and even that looks doubtful. Resentment at the European Community's tardiness to accept new members from East Europe is running high, and is just another sign for many people that they are being treated like second-class citizens in the new order of Europe. The result is a tangible defensiveness and inward-looking attitude which is obstructing any sense there might have been of sharing common cultural ground.

In fact, the old 'us and them' syndrome is being reinforced all the time and as a West European visitor you find yourself fighting feelings of guilt, and defensiveness of a different kind: guilt at your world's shameful hypocrisy and defensiveness against taking personal blame and being treated like a walking money-bag. There are still plenty of people struggling against this debasement of their relationship with each other, but genuine friendship between unequals is very hard, especially when there is little faith that the injustice will be corrected.

It comes as a nasty surprise that democracy does not reward talent, hard work and integrity any more than any other system of government. George Steiner has written that Marxism failed in practice because it overestimated the human capacity for altruism. Having suffered accordingly, the people of Eastern Europe overestimated the greater humanity of democratic, capitalist systems.

In practice, democracy does not mean equal rights, only chance: you might make it and you might not, depending on many things the individual has no control over. Deep confusion and insecurity is the unsurprising result in people newly confronted with this reality, especially since their entire lives were formerly so strictly ordered for them. It is no wonder that resentment is shown against individuals from richer countries, as well as towards those that might be convenient scapegoats, like Gypsies and other minorities.

My ignorance of local history and the Hungarian situation specifically was made very clear to be by Pál, a writer I made contact with via Hungarian PEN. A few years older than myself, he was apparently thoroughly knowledgeable in the historic roots of Central European conflict and wasted no time in letting me know it.

When I told him why I had come to Hungary: to find out if there is a common European culture we could identify with, he snorted with a mixture of amusement and impatience.

'I don't see how you can talk about these things without simply dealing in banalities,' he pronounced.

It was a bad start, and I tried to bring the conversation to a more personal level, to talk about what 1989 had been like for each of us.

'I don't know what I can tell you on that subject,' he said, blocking me again. I began to wonder why he had bothered to meet me at all. He had already made it clear on the telephone that he had little time to spare. And yet he had come, so he must be prepared to talk about something.

'Yes but,' I said, trying to stand my ground, 'personal feelings aren't banal. How do *you* feel? Was 1989 as exciting for you as it was for me and what does it mean to you now?'

My questions seemed to miss the mark, and instead Pál retreated into giving me a history lesson.

'You know, there are other subjects that are much more important to me as a Hungarian. You say you have come along the Danube from Bratislava. Do you know you have just cycled past the object of one of the most contentious issues between Hungary and Slovakia, one that could possibly lead to war?

'No? Well, let me tell you. At Gabčíkovo and Nagymaros on the Danube, there is a huge hydroelectric dam project. [An approximately 120-kilometre stretch of the river, leading up to the Danube Bend.] You didn't notice it? In the seventies it was a joint project between the communist governments of Czechoslovakia and Hungary. It was going to be a showpiece of our modern technology.

'To the opposition and the environmentalists it was always yet another white elephant: huge and ineffective and, worst of all, an ecological disaster. The Hungarian environmentalists campaigned hard in the 1980s, and the building on their side was stopped. Now the communists have gone, and the new Hungarian government has decided to stop funding the project altogether.

'But the Slovaks, on whose territory the dam at Gabčíkovo stands, have succumbed to a different idea. As an emergent national state, they argue that the dam is a matter of national pride and a mark of achievement, which must be continued. If the Hungarians no longer wish to participate then Slovaks must take measures to complete the project alone, which might mean diverting the Danube inland, to where the dam is located.

'However, the international border between Slovakia and Hungary is the middle of the river. It is laid down in the Treaty of Trianon and the Slovaks have no right to change the borders of Hungary. It is an attack on her sovereignty. We may not like the Treaty, but it is what we have.

'Just the other day I heard the Slovak leader say on the radio that Czechs and Hungarians are enemies of Slovak self-determination, and already Hungarians can hear the ancient thunder of nationalist war. [Almost a thousand years of Hungarian domination has by no means been forgotten.] A large minority of Hungarians live in Slovakia. How shall the Hungarian government react if its people under foreign rule are discriminated against? It is the same problem in Romania. Undoubtedly it will give the, as yet, insignificant Hungarian nationalists the rallying call they need to gather substantial support. Ancient hatreds are being resurrected and the flames of ethnocide could easily burst out here too, not just in Bosnia.'

In between the lecture he dropped more significant hints to his thoughts.

'You know, I'm very tired of Westerners asking me to explain what it was like to live under communism – usually in an easy two minutes. What can it mean to you if I say that 1989 means I have the right to go to a demonstration? You cannot know what it means not to have those rights.'

'Yes, but that is exactly why I am here. I would like to know and I have made the effort of coming here to see for myself.'

His manner softened marginally, and I could tell he was trying to readjust his attitude.

'Well,' he tried again, 'what makes you think that a Finnish villager from the Arctic Circle has anything in common with a farmer from Ireland or a fisherman from Corsica?'

Long silence.

'So you think the idea of a European is absurd?' I asked, dejected.

'Yes I do.'

It was hard to swallow, but put so bluntly what do Europeans have in common? Their differences suddenly appeared terribly obvious: language, culture and history.

What about this idea of a culture of Europe, though? But before I had even verbalised the question I realised that I was up against the same thing that had bothered me in Poland, all those weeks ago: the 'Culture of

Europe' is an élitist concept among intellectuals who share the same education. The rest of the population, the vast majority, does not have the benefit of this artificial bond, and has nothing in common – nothing, that is, except their humanity. Yet that is a fact easily obscured, especially in Eastern Europe, where small countries are fighting for their right to exist.

As Pál explained, in this part of the world people find it easier to identify what they are not, rather than what they are. Self-realisation is achieved by defining yourself against something. People are Catholic not Protestant, Liberal not Communist, Czech not Slovak, Hungarian not Serb or Romanian. It is all about divisions. To turn this way of thinking around to seek what one might have in common goes utterly against the grain. What a Hungarian *is* Pál could not tell me.

Another important factor in understanding Eastern Europe is the time warp: all West European countries have fought because of ancient rivalries, and nationalism has done its worst not so long ago. The 'Eastern Bloc', on the other hand, was put under ice by the communists, its conflicts frozen for almost fifty years. Now the ice has gone the old monsters of nationalism and racism are reviving and there are many scores still left to be settled.

Furthermore, these are small countries whose people have had little or no opportunity to establish their identity in the same way as West European peoples. Of course there are exceptions, like the Northern Irish, the Basques or even the Scots. But for the majority of West European countries there is little doubt or insecurity about their French or German or Italian nationhood. Their culture, for all the regional variations and competitive otherness, has been firmly established as a fact of life. People do not suffer from an intrinsic identity crisis.

Yet not so long ago, just over one century ago, Germany and Italy were mere theoretical concepts and the reality was a region full of competing kingdoms, principalities and dukedoms that were only united under one political leadership by force. That force was not always violent, but the unification of those countries was expedient for the most powerful at the time, and so it happened. The First World War had a lot to do with economic rivalry and assertion of political status.

But even now there are people who have never forgotten their enforced loss of nationhood or self-rule. The Irish, Welsh and Scots under English rule are the most obvious examples in Britain, and it is only a few generations ago that the Cornish language finally died out. The war in Northern Ireland is testimony to the fact that there are people in Western Europe, too, who still believe in fighting for self-determination. Communist repression retarded a process in the East that has occurred throughout Europe and is now all the more vicious for having been let loose so suddenly.

Our conversation over a few glasses of wine ended amiably enough, and I felt that we had both learnt something, even if the benefit was mostly mine. By the time we said goodbye he was almost being friendly and, in spite of feeling slightly bruised, I respected him. His defences had been high, but he had given me a chance in the end and shared at least a fraction of his thoughts with me. He had been frank, which is all I could ask for.

However, I found the conversation very depressing. With every week that went by I seemed to have less and less to feel hopeful about. How could I have ever imagined that there was such a person as a European? It had felt so natural to say it: my safe defence against parochial attitudes and prejudice, and the bedrock of my faith in humanism as the best set of ideas.

How different my feelings now, compared to the exhilaration I had felt when the Berlin Wall came down. I believed then that I would be one of the lucky ones, finding it easier to adapt to a new European identity because of my mixed ancestry. Never did I feel such a sense of hope and excitement about the future as during my visit to Berlin for the New Year's Eve of 1989/1990. I imagined that it was the beginning of a new decade and so much more besides, and had wanted to be at the very epicentre of it all.

Then, I had found the streets of Berlin full of people with the same idea as me, come from all over Europe and even beyond, mostly young people. Along the Wall itself there was the chip, chip, chip sound of countless hammers and chisels making their own blow for freedom and a coveted piece of Wall. Most valued of all were pieces with graffiti on them, and already there were stalls where men, women and children stood over piles of rubble and chips, selling them for anything from 1 DM to 20 DM, depending on size and quality of graffiti marks. Trade was booming, but I felt it was cheating to buy a piece, and swiftly grabbed some falling chips from a hammer up a ladder. It was a free-for-all and everyone was taking what they could get. (It never occurred to me that it was a sign of things to come: the wholesale selling off and take-over of East Germany which would leave large numbers of East Germans unemployed, and many more as second-class citizens.)

On New Year's Eve itself, some friends and I went to one of the thousands of parties that were heaving in Berlin that night. This one was in an old office block, a large open-plan floor creating the atmosphere of a warehouse party. Bare walls were covered in fresh graffiti and dim lights showed figures standing in clouds of smoke. The scene could have been a party of young people anywhere in the West, except that there were young East Germans here too, and perhaps even some Hungarians, Poles and Czechs. I had found myself eyeing them with a certain curiosity – as if East Germans would somehow look different. But they were dressed just like anyone else might have been, and the only difference was in their accents, if they were from beyond Berlin, and a certain insecurity that could equally have been shown by anyone feeling a bit nervous at a party full of strangers. East and West skirted each other, invisible barriers between clusters of *Ossies* and *Wessies*. But as the night wore on the mixing got less self-conscious and the irrepressible excitement of the occasion carried us all into the dawning hours of 1990.

I didn't reach the Wall and the Brandenburg Gate until the first hour of daylight, by which time the millions had gone. It was a shame to have missed the excitement here. On the other hand, the crush must have been terrifying, and later in the day the news spread that people had, in fact, been crushed to death under a collapsing bandstand. Better to be here now, the silence still loud from the recent crowd, yet the solitary hour allowing a very private moment of reflection. How could it have been that this man-made division seemed so permanent all our lives? And now it was gone. Just like that. It was still a stupendous thought.

Only the boulevards leading to the Gate were crowded with Trabants and Western cars, windows steamed up from the sleeping bodies inside. Berlin was full and many had to sleep on the freezing streets and in the parks, or in their cars if they had them. A couple of East German guards wandered up and down on their side of the Wall, saying nothing when some youths clambered up the forbidden concrete. Close by there was an actual gap in the Wall where you could step into the old no man's land. What a thrill to squeeze through into the emptiness and see the old watch-towers. Was there really no one who was going to shoot? Old fears die hard, but how wonderful to be still young at this time, with a whole lifetime to see the new Europe unfurl. It was a moment of pure joy.

Three years later, my experiences on this journey were forcing me to reassess my definitions. If there is no such person as a European, what should I think of myself as from now on? Being a half-breed of two cultures I could not retreat back to a simple answer and my sense of loss was extremely disorientating. Ever since I could think for myself I had clung to this idea, and what 1989 had meant to me, more than anything else, was that at last I would be part of a new culture where nationality was unimportant.

Now the illusion of 'Europe' was rapidly fading despite my best efforts to deny it and I was as confused as the rest of them. Worse still, the profound divisions between nationalities that this journey was showing up cracked the foundations of the closest thing to faith I had: the belief in a common humanity that transcends differences of culture, religion and language. If this idea holds no water in Eastern Europe, why should it be relevant anywhere else? In which case, 'We're doomed,' as one of my friends likes to say, and for the first time I suspected he was right all along.

A snide critic once said that a travel writer is a person with 'a hole in the soul; someone who is by definition looking for something, and not smart enough to settle for religion.' It is a sentence as clever and amusing as it is sterile and heartless. I wish I could settle for religion. It would be a great relief. Instead I think I might go the Hungarian way and start defining myself by what I am not: I am a travel writer not a journalist! Actor not critic.

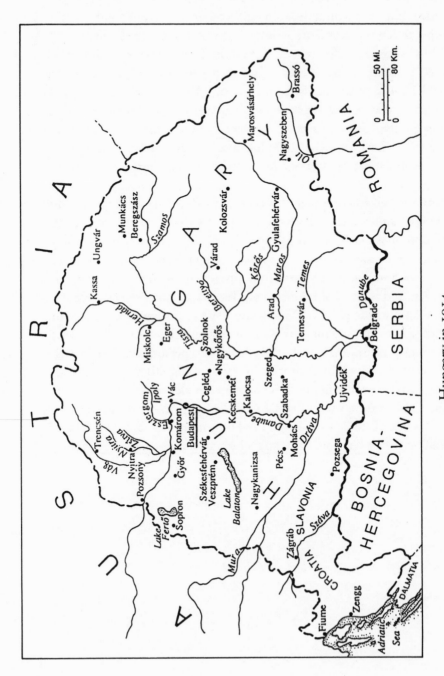

Hungary in 1914

From: *A History of Hungary*, P.F. Sugar et al, London, I.B. Tauris & Co., 1990

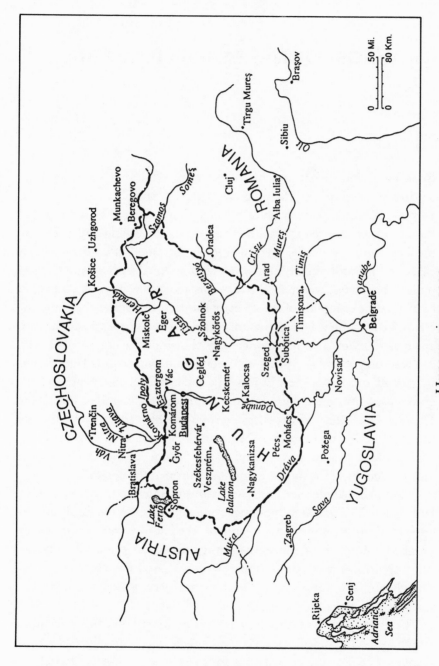

Hungary since 1920

From: *A History of Hungary*, P.F. Sugar et al, London, I.B. Tauris & Co., 1990

FROM BUDAPEST TO KELEBIA

Budapest is big, black and heavy to digest. It leaves you physically exhausted, even in small helpings, though that probably has a lot to do with the pollution. After a day in the city your skin and hair is filthy, and the air you breathe is sooty with fumes from the heaving traffic. Due to the local terrain of nearby hills, the capital also often suffers from what is called 'temperature inversion', when cold polluted air becomes trapped under a blanket of warm air above. Years ago, we were told, you could hardly see the other side of the street for the darkened atmosphere, but the city still has a long way to go before ceasing to be a serious health hazard, and it was a relief to escape to our campsite beyond the northern suburbs.

I was sorry to feel like this. I had been looking forward to Budapest. It is, after all, one of the great European capitals and I imagined it as a large and elegant city, grand with imperial architecture lining the banks of the Danube. I had seen photos of the huge neo-Gothic parliament built along the water's edge, reminiscent of Westminster Palace, and I had expected a similar effect. Instead, it was simply large: '879 feet long, 408 feet wide, and 315 feet high', as tourist guides have droned for decades.

In fact, the whole city impresses with its dimensions, but somehow lacks grace. The size of its buildings commands respect but rarely admiration, and the monstrous architecture of the last forty years, periodically plonked among the nineteenth-century streetscapes and city squares, often spoils the most picturesque places. Beyond the centre, the city sprawls out in a confusion of belching industry, wastelands and poor housing that never encourages a backward glance.

The great boulevards that stretch out into a rigid nineteenth-century design in central Budapest send you looking for the nearest bus stop, their seemingly endless distances discouraging any idea of walking. One such is

Andrassy avenue, almost two miles long – and thankfully not called Népkoztársaság any more – which ends in the intimidating Heroes' Square, where a giant half-moon colonnade stands filled with statues to the greater glory of Hungarian history.

Knowing its significance, I tried to feel an appropriate reverence for this particular spot, but it was no good. The stone columns and statues did not breathe any of the excitement and pathos of the momentous events they had witnessed, like the recent reburial of Hungary's General Secretary, Imre Nagy. He was hanged after the 1956 Uprising against communism, and had lain in an unmarked grave for thirty-one years before being given a proper state funeral in 1989. The ceremony took place here, at Heroes' Square, but the heady atmosphere was long gone.

After meeting Pál I was possibly not in the right frame of mind to enjoy Budapest. The melancholy and pent-up anger I had encountered here affected my perception. Yet it would be wrong to say there was nothing I enjoyed. We spent some good times exploring the city by its trams and buses and, best of all, riding the old funicular which climbs the steep ascent to the royal quarter on Buda's Castle Hill. (Buda was the earliest settlement, growing up on the right bank of the Danube, while Pest developed later, on the other side, the two only united into one city in 1873.)

The view from the former royal terrace is striking, the height and distance giving the city the image of splendour its architects intended. Far below, the Danube cuts between the busy Pest district stretching out on the flat east bank, while hilly Buda rises to the west, its high plateau crammed with rebuilt medieval buildings behind ancient fortifications. The great palace too is a restored shell of its last incarnation as an eighteenth-century residence, since almost all the buildings here were destroyed in the last war. Even before then the royal seat was repeatedly devastated, most effectively by the Turks, in 1541, who ruled over central Hungary for almost 150 years. Nothing remains to remind of them now except the numerous Turkish baths still operating around the city.

How different the city must have looked after the Ottoman ruler, Suleiman the Magnificent, sent his appointed pasha to govern here. The skyline then would have been dominated by mosques, with countless minarets proclaiming the new religion each day. Next to the mosques, the great bazaar would have been the thriving heart of the city, protected by a building of almost equal size and importance as the central mosque, where merchants kept their most precious goods, brought from all over the empire.

From Buda the main route 'home' for the Turks was via Belgrade and Niš, then on to the Bulgarian city of Sofia, south-east to Plovdiv and Edirne, and finally to Istanbul, which was the major crossroads for all Ottoman trade routes. It was this route, too, that the Turkish military once used to reach the Hungarian 'province'. Today only history books bear witness to these ancient highways, their path apparently as empty of tangible evidence as much of my own historic route, which had gone distinctly cold for the moment.

The Magyar inhabitants under Turkish rule would have found themselves referred to as *zimmi*, meaning a person who is protected and enjoys religious freedom because he accepts the Moslem state. But the majority seem to have preferred to flee, and the history books record that by 1547, only 1,000 Christians remained in the city.

It took until 1686 to oust the foreign rulers from Buda, when they were successfully routed by a combined European force of 65,000 soldiers. Even then it took another thirteen years to get rid of them altogether, and the result for the Hungarians was not as good as they might have wished, for now they found themselves ruled by the Habsburgs instead. It was they who last rebuilt the royal palace of Buda, under the auspices of one of their most famous rulers: the Empress Maria Theresa.

The Castle Hill quarter today is on a more accessible scale than the austere elegance of the lower city, the medieval and baroque buildings more beautiful and welcoming. Quaint arches and crooked doorways lead to quiet courtyards on three parallel streets, and only the orange glass box of the local Hilton disturbs an otherwise historic scene.

It squats directly opposite the Mátyás church, whose interior overwhelms the eye with coloured patterns on every conceivable surface. Columns, ceilings and walls are painted in the rich tones and plenty of gold that all medieval churches were once decorated with, but this was the first time I had seen an example of it. The reason was that this church is actually a nineteenth-century recreation of the original, and for modern tastes the effect as a whole is much too busy with patterns and colour. Dark and heavy, it is as hard to digest as the city itself. Nevertheless, it was interesting to see what you otherwise have to remember to imagine when looking at medieval interiors. All those bare stone walls and columns would always have been embellished.

This and the bars of the south-western district made our trips into town worthwhile, but we were not tempted to come more than a few times. The city did not ask to be liked and we did not stay long to try. Looking back I wish I had. We only scraped the surface of Budapest, which is undoubtedly the kind of place made by its people rather than its physical features. Then again, there is no reason to like a place just because one imagined one would, and in this case I didn't much. Perhaps it had something to do with the impenetrable language as well, which, as one writer put it, makes the traveller feel 'a little more superfluous than usual'.

At any rate, the city's people were deeply preoccupied and the local press reflected the confusion of the time. One of the strangest reports was about an American Independence Day celebration that took place on Margit Island, in the middle of the Danube. The reporter related how a Hungarian friend of his could not help wondering why this celebration had been organised: 'Russians out, Americans in?' he asked among the star-spangled banners.

A similar question has haunted Hungary for centuries. Does it belong to the East or the West, historically, culturally, and politically? Do the three necessarily have to come under the same heading? How about a bit of this and a bit of that, choosing the best of both worlds? Shall the newly free Hungary belong to the European Common Market or the Black Sea Economic Union being established by Turkey? It is already a partner of the Visegrad Three: the economic and political association between Poland, Czecho-Slovakia and itself.

And all this does not even touch the difficult issue of the Hungarian minorities in Slovakia, Romania and Serbia, and what stand should be taken on that. Hungary's new constitution declares that the government rules in the name of *all* Hungarians, so intervention outside its borders on behalf of ethnic Hungarians is certainly possible.

Another thorny question is the response to be made to the huge influx of refugees just beginning to arrive from former Yugoslavia, estimated in the local press at 50,000 in July 1992, compared with only 8,000 allowed into Britain by December 1992. (Meanwhile, Austria had taken in at least 60,000 by this time, Switzerland 50,000, Germany 200,000, and many other European countries had accepted around 75,000 people each.)

Then there are the waves of immigrants from the East, many of whom appear set to remain in Hungary permanently because no Western country will accept them and returning home is often impossible. For a small nation that tends to see itself surrounded by hostile races the prospect of being swamped by foreigners takes on particular significance, quite apart from the fact that the local economy cannot sustain an increased social security bill. (Hungary's population stands at around 10 million, including an estimated 40,000 Romanians and 355,000 Gypsies, as well as much smaller minorities of Germans, Slovaks, Croats and Serbs. All except the Gypsies are granted recognition and run their own institutions.)

The country was once the privileged one amongst the Eastern Bloc captives, with the best food and clothing. Now Hungary is an economic cripple like all the rest and insecurity and confusion magnifies many fears, especially here. With a war raging on its southern border and potential conflict with both Slovakia and Romania brewing on its northern and eastern border, it is no wonder a siege mentality is developing and, without substantial Western aid, Hungary could easily develop a full-blown case of violent paranoia, increasing the pressure in an already volatile region.

Back at Üröm was another world. Behind the screening hedges and willow trees of the campsite, predominantly Danes and Germans enjoyed the good services of Juliusz, each settled on their little territory of grass, where invisible mental boundaries marked the limits within which sun-beds, bicycles and camping tables could spread.

There was a definite proprietorial settler mentality among the long-term residents and annual regulars, and newcomers by no means gained instant recognition. After a day or two, however, we were already on nodding terms with the friendly Danish couple next to us, and they benevolently lent wine glasses when they saw us drinking out of plastic. 'Such a shame to drink wine like that,' she said, and we were happy to accept.

Most people here were in camper vans or even mobile homes, complete with porcelain and cutlery, tables and chairs, and all culinary mod cons. We were paupers by comparison, sitting on the ground outside our tent or at the public table, each with just one plastic plate, cup and steel eating utensils. We were not even camping properly by the others' standards, being the only ones who were using the free kitchen to cook at.

Keeping up with the neighbours was as rampant here as in any suburb. Each evening the site's residents went on a stroll around the gravel path, surreptitiously spying on the others' equipment while bidding 'Good evening' and 'Wasn't it another lovely day today?'. Men scoffed at their neighbour's clumsy parking and wives shook their heads over the badly behaved children next-door.

It was extraordinary to me the lengths to which some people had gone to bring their domesticity with them. And not only that, but the way the women seemed to be expected to carry on with their housewifely duties, just as if they were at home. It seemed to me there was hardly any point in coming if they still had to cook and wash and clean the caravan each day. I did envy the couple across the path, though, where the wife put out a fresh tablecloth each morning and produced percolated coffee, and home-made jam with fresh rolls.

The gadgets that seemed to be standard equipment for modern camping opened up a whole new world to me: collapsible washing-lines, portable stairs to step in and out of caravans, plastic washing-bowls for dishes and clothes, or even hand-turned, portable washing-barrels, the closest thing to a proper machine. Most astounding of all were our neighbours to the other side, whose luxury caravan not only had an aerial, but a satellite dish as well.

The owners were a middle-aged couple, who seemed to have acquired a young child just before it was too late, and their five-year-old daughter led them a merry dance from dawn till dusk. The poor father hardly had time to watch his multi-channel television. 'When are you going to start listening to your father?' came the repeated complaint from behind the net curtain, followed by an accelerating howl stopped only with more food. The child was grotesquely fat and quite unappreciative of all the efforts her harassed parents went to. It was domestic hell transplanted abroad, and at what a cost to purse and nerves.

New arrivals had to tread carefully, making sure they did not encroach on someone else's patch, not to mention their view. One morning a couple of young men parked far too close to our Danish neighbour's vehicle, and I waited expectantly for a showdown. They froze over their breakfast, and silent glances communicated what their children could only guess at. But there was no spectacle that morning. They were reasonable people, so they did not immediately charge out and ask for the offending vehicle to be moved. Instead the wife went to have a quiet word with Juliusz, and by late afternoon the van had moved.

The next morning it was our turn to feel imposed upon. A group of twelve Austrian motorcyclists had arrived the night before, and now they were eating breakfast at the only public table available, *our* table, as we thought, since we had been the only ones using it until then. How quickly you adapt! We sat on the grass over our porridge and pretended not to notice the indignity in best British style. But we laughed as well. It was time to leave before we became completely soft.

Surrounded by all these efficient campers we were finally shamed into trying our own cooker. After all, Benoît had been carrying it in his pannier for many weeks now, so we felt we really ought to use it. The trouble was that neither of us had the nerve to try. Benoît had never used such a thing and I had completely forgotten the procedure, even though I had spent months with an identical model only three years before.

Between us we are not very effective when it comes to practical matters. (We had only just figured out the bicycles, though not the purpose of half the tools we had brought.) Benoît could not remember which fuel valve he had fixed on to the cooker in London, and I was terrified the thing would blow up in our faces if we used the wrong fuel.

We reread the instructions and compared impressions on what it meant. I knew all about pumping air into the fuel, the most important lesson I remembered from my last experience and, at last, we held our breath and put a match to the petrol gas. Orange blue flames shot out at once and we marvelled at it, as if we had never seen such a thing. 'It's easy,' we told each other with relief.

It is so silly to be frightened of technical things, and in my case there was no excuse at all. Of course I knew how to use the cooker, but somehow I did not have the confidence to remember, and we had to come this far before I decided to try. Better late than never! From now on, though, we were going to camp *and* cook, which was just as well because we were going to need all our new skills very soon.

The morning we broke camp a fine drizzle descended from a milky sky, and we struggled against a lethargic will and reluctant muscles. Having settled here so comfortably it was difficult to decide to set off, especially when the weather promised a wet and windy day, and we had no certain destination to aim for. We were simply heading south along the Danube, ever closer to the Serbian border and an even more uncertain future. But we rolled up the tent, packed our bags, dug out the plastic rain covers, and finally cycled into Budapest at midday, a huge obstacle course in our path there was no way of avoiding.

Cycling in cities is a treacherous business at the best of times, but especially so when you cannot understand the road signs nor easily ask for directions. Street maps do not usually include the suburbs, while country maps simply mark cities as an irregular blob, making navigation off the major motorways very haphazard indeed. Most times we just had to guess and hope for the best which, until now, had worked fine, since none of the towns and cities had been very large. Today was the exception, and it took us three hours just to cross the city and find the right road the other side.

Somewhere on the southern edges of Budapest we became inextricably lost in a tangle of junctions and motorway entrances, ending up at a windswept truck stop on the main highway heading south-east. We were completely off course and a gang of hoary Turkish truck drivers eyed us with amusement: two wet cyclists dwarfed by giant lorries, quite obviously lost. As I approached them they lent back in their chairs, rubbing huge bellies in anticipation, and I wished I was not wearing exposing cycling pants. '*Sprechen Sie Deutsch?*' I asked hopefully, and soon I had them arguing over which was the best way to connect with the road heading in a more southerly direction. 'Left a short way, over that bridge in the distance, then under the motorway and along for a few kilometres ... anyway that way', was as accurate a direction as I could get, and we set off once more, cursing, sweaty and splashed by traffic.

By the time we found country road 51 the sky had taken on a nasty shade of lead, unleashing ominous heavy drops that quickly turned into pelting rain. A proper gale whipped up and we ran to take cover under a sheltered train stop. It was a black mid-afternoon by now. We had barely escaped the clutches of the city and it was tempting to take a train to the first town with a hotel. Instead we waited for the rain to let up and just carried on, past the sodden corpse of a recently killed dog, lured into the distance by a sign promising a luxury campsite in fifteen kilometres.

What a relief it was to be out of the city at last – away from the busy traffic and sure of the direction. Our mood lifted with the weather, and a new surge of energy sent us recklessly past the first campsite and on to the next one, marked on our map by a place called Dömsöd.

We were, in fact, not travelling along the main body of the river at all, but along a side channel that embraces the huge island of Csepel, dividing the Danube just south of Budapest. The island is about 50 kilometres long, and the small town of Dömsöd nestles just across from its eastern bank, with a seemingly endless row of holiday cottages built along the riverside. Many of them were built of wood, hardly larger than a garden shed, but each had a neat patch of garden and their own jetty for sunbathing and fishing. (This from the same river that annually receives around 9,000 litres of sulphuric acid from the chemical works at Bratislava alone!)

Cycling along the narrow track at sunset, the scene was all rural tranquillity: willows brushed the glassy water, men sat patiently waiting for their evening catch, and the only sounds came from laughing children and birds among the treetops. Everything glistened in the orange light of the setting sun, still wet from the stormy afternoon, though no longer buffeted by angry winds. It had been a long hard day, but when we checked into the waterside camping ground at last, we felt happy and at peace.

The tent was up in expert time and we did not even mind the lukewarm showers. In complete contrast to our recent home, we were the only people at this site, perhaps because it was new and unknown, and our only disturbance came from the incessant buzz of mosquitoes. So close to water they were everywhere. Soon each of us had dozens of itchy welts and we took care not to leave the inner tent zip open for too long. It only takes one insect whining in your ear to drive you to raging madness, which can end up pretty destructive inside the fragile walls of a small tent.

Next morning we ate the best *lángos* of the entire journey, soaked in garlic and cheese and washed down by heart-stopping coffee, and set off into the Hungarian plain: the *puszta*. It was not the most direct route, but current events had overtaken the amber trail, and I decided to head south-east instead of directly along the river, because of an article I had read in *Budapest Week*. If I could find no evidence of the amber past for the time being, at least I could discover something about the present.

The article described a Bosnian refugee camp close to the Serbian border, where 1,600 people had reputedly arrived during the last week. It said a tent reception centre had been set up in the village of Kelebia, the first Hungarian railway station after the border, and reported stories of Bosnian Muslims forced out of their homes, sent away with nothing but the clothes on their back and a one-way ticket to Hungary. To make a detour via this village seemed like the ideal opportunity to hear the Bosnian side before we entered Serbia, and I hoped somehow I would be allowed access and find someone who spoke either German or English.

We were both nervous about the prospect of entering what remained of Federal Yugoslavia. The United Nations had imposed its sanctions, so our countries were declared enemies of Serbia, and there was talk in the press of a possible military strike against her. For all we knew we were cycling straight into a war and neither of us felt good about it. Even without the war spreading to Serbian territory, we hardly expected a warm welcome. This diversion, then, was not just a worthwhile cause, but also a subconscious delaying tactic: more time to think about what we were doing and possible alternatives.

But first we had to get to Kelebia, a journey that was going to take us two days of cycling across the flat Hungarian plain, and so we struck east, following empty country lanes into the abandoned countryside – or so it felt. Perhaps it really is. Sixty per cent of the population is classed as urban in Hungary and the capital acts like a magnet, especially these days, since the economy is in ruins.

Occasionally horse-drawn carts clip-clopped by with loads of coal or fresh hay and, every now and then, we passed through a small village, where headscarfed countrywomen stared at us with bemused interest. There seemed to be no young people at all, and the tiny squares before the churches were sadly empty. Claudio Magris described the region well when he said that 'in this empty, uncaring landscape, life flows negligently by, moving towards infinite distance like a herd of cattle. The only thing that happens is that time passes.' The very air is turgid with nothingness.

Again we were soaked by rain, and the endless rows of sunflowers outside the villages bowed their heads as if to hide. Strung up to our noses in rain gear we seemed to be pedalling nowhere, the flat horizon ever distant. I tried not to dwell on the wet plastic sticking to my neck and arms, the synthetic material creating an unwelcome heat in this humid weather.

Puszta means 'abandoned' or 'bleak' in Hungarian, and no wonder. Yet once it was a fertile plateau covered by forests and busy with serfs working for the huge estates of the nobility. But when the Turks conquered Hungary the entire region was depopulated by a combination of over a century of war and a policy of deforestation to make the area easier to police. The result is a historic example of environmental destruction, which turned a massive area of land (almost 46,000 square kilometres) into a swamp that only became useful as grassland in the nineteenth century, when effective drainage was established.

It is from that era, the last century, that the most famous Hungarian images originate: the galloping horsemen with whirling swords and billowing trousers, and whitewashed homesteads hung with the flaming red of dried paprika, the country's national spice. Sadly we never saw anything so dramatic or picturesque. Instead we spent the night in the small town of Kiskörös, in a hotel that doubled up as the local strip joint, and hurried on the next day to reach Kelebia, a further 50 kilometres south-east.

The village turned out to be a two-street affair bisected by the railway tracks with nothing interesting going on at all. At first we thought the camp must be on the edge of the village somewhere, and we cycled a short distance in every direction. But the only person we met was an itinerant chimney-sweep, his brushes wrapped around his shoulder and the contours of his face a greasy map of sooty lines.

Back in the village, people seemed to be entirely unaware that there could be a refugee camp of over a thousand Bosnians here. Some shrugged their shoulders and pleaded ignorance. Others denied there was such a place, while the railway staff treated us with grave suspicion. Eventually, however, one of the men admitted that there had been a reception centre, but that it had only been for transit passengers heading elsewhere. In fact, the official said, the government had closed down the camp.

Could all trace of such a place disappear in just a few days? Had the journalist made up his story? Or did the people here want to deny the camp's existence for some reason? It was impossible to tell, but the atmosphere was decidedly edgy and clearly there was a reluctance to speak with strangers, especially ones asking too many questions. It had been a long shot in the first place, and we reluctantly gave up on finding anything, let alone a refugee to talk to.

In the end we did find about eight military tents with mattresses behind the railway station. Actually it was the back garden of the station house, the green military canvas camouflaged under shading trees. There was no one there, however, not even a soldier, and so we left, sure that we had not discovered anything, and feeling rather cheated. We were just a few kilometres from the Serbian border now, and there was nothing for it but to carry on.

Rain soaked us yet again while we cycled through some rare forest. The road took us straight past a secluded military base, but we had the sense not to stop and visit there. It had been naive to imagine that we would find out anything. Even if refugees were being kept at the base hidden in the forest, there had probably never been any chance that two foreigners without journalistic credentials would have been granted an interview. A combination of wishful thinking and genuine interest had led us astray.

Like so much of our time in Hungary, the last day was full of anticipation unrewarded and, although I was uncertain about crossing the next frontier, there was at least the excitement of heading into the unknown. We cycled in silence, each of us mulling over the day's non-event, bracing ourselves for whatever might happen, which was perhaps going to be nothing at all.

4. SERBIA

Race instinct, one of the strongest of the human passions, has as yet shown no tendency to die out anywhere. It seems, therefore, a little unreasonable to expect the Balkan peoples to be the ones to set an example to the rest of the world by dropping all international jealousies and national aspirations.

International jealousy is certainly at the root of the present grievous condition of affairs in the Balkans, but it is the jealousy not only of the Balkan people but that of other nations which are supposed to be older and wiser and whose quarrels are of even longer standing.

Mary Edith Durham,
Through the Lands of the Serb, 1904

LAND AT WAR

'Serbia good, OK!' said the border guard, and we smiled falsely. So this was it. We were in evil Serbia, a country at war with its Croatian and Bosnian brothers and sisters. The Moslems too are Serbs or Croats, converted centuries ago by the Turkish overlords, and they must be one of very few peoples identified by their religion, not their race. (The phrase 'ethnic cleansing' is therefore a misnomer, since virtually everyone directly involved in the war is Slav.)

Yet few Bosnian Moslems remember their original Slav names, given up generations ago as part of their conversion to Islam. It was the turn of the fifteenth century, a time when most people lived in abject servitude to the nobility, so it was no wonder that the majority of converts were peasants, who pragmatically adopted the new religion in order to enjoy a better life under their Moslem masters. A crucial factor, for example, was that only Moslems could own land. As one historian put it: 'In Europe conversion was limited pretty much to certain elements who had really never understood or practised their faith correctly and for whom, therefore, apostasy was less a question of belief than of convenience.' Folk Christianity was replaced by folk Islam and, over the centuries, many Bosnian Moslems became wealthy landowners, members of their families taking up leading positions in society as well.

Once the Turks had been expelled – almost five hundred years later – all was reasonably fine as long as there was no question of territorial partitions. (In other words, no question of the landed élite giving up their privileges and possessions.) The Bosnian Moslems are said to have worn their religion like a useful jacket, taken off whenever it was not needed and therefore never a cause for conflict with their non-Moslem neighbours. But the relationship was fundamentally damaged by the Second

World War, when the majority of Bosnian Moslems sided with the Croat fascists. According to the BBC correspondent, Misha Glenny, in many regions of Bosnia-Hercegovina four Serbs died for every Moslem killed.

Under Tito, the Moslems were elevated from a minority to an officially recognised Yugoslav nation, on a par with Serbs, Croats, Slovenes and Macedonians, and therein lies the basis of the present claim for an independent state of Bosnia-Hercegovina. It is also said that since 1990, fundamentalists have infested the Bosnian Moslems, just like in similar societies around the world, and their leader, Alija Izetbegović, is said to have begged support from Iran and Libya to help fight for a Moslem state in Europe.

A Moslem state in Europe! As a concept it is anathema to many and worth denying by war – at least from the present political leaders' point of view. And who is to say that is not exactly what other Western leaders believe as well? It is for that reason that the Serbs, who see themselves as the historic saviours of Europe from the Turks and Islam, cannot understand why their cause is not being supported by the West. It is just one angle of countless others regarding this war, many of which were to be presented to us with equal force.

As early as 1904, the travel writer Mary Edith Durham wrote that '... either party seizes upon the stranger and tries to prevent his views being "prejudiced". He seldom has need to complain that he has heard one side only; but there is a Catholic side, an Orthodox side, a Mohammedan side, there are German, Slav, Italian, Turkish and Albanian sides; and when he has heard them all he feels far less capable of forming an opinion on the Eastern Question than he did before.'

But on that first day we had heard neither the questions nor the answers and only had media-filled imaginations to taunt our nerves. Our main source of information until now had been the BBC World Service on Benoît's short-wave radio, so we knew few details, only that the conflict was getting worse all the time.

Some drivers honked at us in passing, as if to say 'Right on!'. A boy held up the two-fingered peace sign as we passed, shouting 'Serbia OK!'. We were not sure if we liked this kind of welcome, however, even if it was quite the opposite of what we had expected. We did not think of ourselves as sympathisers with the Serbs and were rather embarrassed to be treated as such. But it seemed that our mere presence here proved that we must be on their side, and we were welcomed with hearty enthusiasm. Far from being the objects of suspicion, we were regarded as the glorious exception to all those misguided Western tourists who had deserted Serbia that summer.

The first town we came to was Subotica, and we cycled into the centre in search of lunch. Could this really be a country at war? It seemed incredible, but the place had an easy-going, Mediterranean atmosphere. Pedestrian avenues were sprinkled with clusters of outdoor cafés. Stripy parasols fluttered together like large bunches of flowers, and the tables were full of people enjoying a drink in the sunshine. Music flooded the pavement with different tunes every few steps, there was laughter, and men eyeing foxy women from behind reflecting sunglasses. No one seemed to be in any particular hurry and the scene was reminiscent of Spain or Italy.

It seemed hardly possible that this country had only recently emerged from the drab era of communism. Obviously former Yugoslavia was an exceptional State. Nevertheless, we were surprised to find ourselves among relaxed and confident people who showed none of the psychic scars in their faces, so common in Poland or Hungary.

Nobody bothered us or stared as we pushed our bikes among the shoppers, and when we found a suitable place for having a meal, the menu was even bilingual: in Serbo-Croat and German. Well, of course – Yugoslavia has long been a favourite holiday destination, and the waiter greeted us with urbane sophistication. A teenager came to admire our bikes, and we traded 'bike talk' on the pros and cons of touring cycles versus mountain bikes.

This was certainly no backward place. This was a country that felt naturally close to my experience of southern European culture and it was as if we were out of Eastern Europe and into the Mediterranean, a region with all the exuberance, openness and volatility associated with Latin cultures. Those were my first impressions – soon to be tempered by the experience of trying to find somewhere to stay, later in the day. Everything was not as easy and accessible as it seemed that first morning, and the state of the country was far from ordinary.

The war between Serbs and Croats had begun over a year ago by the time we arrived. The war in Bosnia-Hercegovina had been raging for over four months, and United Nations sanctions against what was now being referred to as 'rump' Yugoslavia, firmly branded Serbia (as well as Montenegro, the other state remaining in the Federal Republic of Yugoslavia), and the Serb-dominated federal army, as the aggressor. As a result, by the summer of 1992, tourists were naturally shunning the region, and in particular Serbia.

Only a few foreign vehicles were still using the overland route to holidays in Greece and Turkey – via Serbia and Macedonia, since the motorway from Zagreb to Belgrade was in the war zone – and the only other foreigners travelling this way were Greek and Turkish lorry drivers. The majority were filling up with petrol in Hungary and then driving through in one long haul, at most making one overnight stop before crossing the next international border.

Serbian hotels and guest houses therefore stood empty and, when an occasional customer did arrive, the manager wanted strictly Deutsch-marks, and not less than 100 DM either, to make up for lost business. This put accommodation firmly beyond our reach and no amount of haggling could persuade anyone to give us a room after our first day's cycling. They were used to German tourists, for whom a one-off payment of 100 DM for the night was the least of their worries, so bargaining was impossible. Unfortunately there were no campsites on this part of our route either.

Eventually, after cycling much further than we had intended, exhaus-ted and worried about approaching darkness, we pulled into a roadside restaurant for supper and ordered a meal of stuffed peppers and a bottle of wine. If we were going to sleep rough the least we could do was eat well first.

The food was delicious and the bottle of *Banatski* was the best dry white wine we had tasted so far. Milan, the proprietor, was pleased we liked his wife's cooking and, being able to chat in German, he told us a little about how business was tough right now. Only the truck drivers and tourists buses were regulars these days, and he shook his head at the thought of them.

'The Turkish buses are the worst. They stop here and then the passengers shit in my garden!' he told me indignantly. 'They use this place for a toilet, but I keep a gun behind the counter and as soon as I see them pulling up, I tell them to get out.

'We are civilised people', he said, as if we three were obviously of common stock. We smiled non-commitally, and I plucked up the courage to ask if we could pitch our tent on his land. At least this way we would not risk trespassing or causing undue attention.

'Well, if you can find a patch that suits you go ahead,' he agreed, and we gratefully wheeled our bikes through the long grass and into a small copse of trees.

It was not the best of places. Crumpled toilet paper hung among the blades, and the small patch of level ground we found was riddled with deep burrows of who knows what kind of animal. But we had found somewhere safe to stay and that was all that mattered. In the morning we could wash at the restaurant's sink and fill up our water-bottles, so things were not too bad and we slept very well.

The route we were following next morning was a single-lane country road but, because of the unusual circumstances, there was a steady stream of thunderous lorries, trucks and buses, all in a hurry and paying little attention to cyclists. If there was a speed limit no one was taking any notice of it, and huge juggernauts shot past, wrenching our handlebars with every gust left in their wake.

It was a nerve-racking business cycling in these conditions, but going around corners was positively dangerous. High up in their cabins, the drivers could easily ignore us and, on one particular bend, a container lorry cut the corner so tight I was forced off the road altogether. I just ran out of space: cut off by deadly steel whipping past my body, a hair's breadth from disaster, leaving no choice but to crash into a ditch, Benoît following close behind, only just managing to avoid piling on top of me. No one stopped.

Had the lorry and I touched the result does not bear thinking about, but there was no physical damage to either body or bicycle, and I just stood there, trembling with shock. All strength was suddenly gone from my arms and legs and my words got stuck like a scratched record: 'I could have been killed! I could have been killed! He never stopped, the bastard. He never stopped, the bastard. He never stopped ...' Benoît's response was more internal, but his face had gone an ashy yellow colour.

We stopped at the first roadside café we could find, but the waiter was surly and rude, so we left. By the time we found a better place I sat crying into my coffee, the unpleasant waiter from before a catalyst for my tears. But it was the release I needed and soon I was all right. The road split off where the motorway began, and at last we cycled in peace and I could notice the flowers along the roadside for the first time: here it was pink thistles, a lovely shade of old rose.

Novi Sad, capital of the Vojvodina plain, was our first base in Serbia; a modern town embracing an ancient centre on the banks of the Danube, 30 kilometres east of the Croatian border. A huge fortress thrones on a promontory opposite the town, where attractively dilapidated streets present a faded nineteenth-century film set below its walls. The gas streetlamps still hang on their cast-iron frames, but none work, and many of the crumbling houses are abandoned, their ancient window-panes hung with dusty spiders' webs.

Also on this side of the Danube is the village of Sremska Kamenica, where we found ourselves a room with the superb luxury of not only a private bath and double bed, but also a spacious balcony overlooking the river at just the right spot for watching the setting sun slip over a watery horizon. The bathroom even had a sauna attached, but it did not work and neither of us would have used it anyway.

What bliss after weeks and weeks of aching backs from sleeping either in the tent or lumpy single beds. (Double beds are almost unheard of in Eastern European guest houses.) Hot water too! All this was no small prize – especially not for a mere US$8 – and we immediately decided to stay at least two nights. We were to discover why the place was so cheap only later...

It suited us to linger anyway, because the Croatian town of Vukovar was just 80 kilometres upriver, and we wanted to try and reach it if we could. One of the first places to be utterly destroyed in the war, we had read in British papers that tourists now went there on excursions. No less morbid and curious, we wanted to go too. Neither of us had ever experienced a war and we wanted to see what a bombed-out city looked like. Perhaps we could make up for our failure to learn anything about the war in Kelebia, and it seemed a more likely prospect than finding information on the area's links with the historic amber trade.

Wary now of newspaper reports, we checked with the local tourist office to see if it really was all right to go to Vukovar and, if so, how. The woman there showed no surprise at our wish. In fact, it was as if she was totally unaware that there was a war going on – at least that is how she behaved.

'Would it be possible to go to Vukovar?' we tentatively asked.

'Sure. No problem,' she replied.

We had to press her to phone the police, just to make sure, but even they said it was all right as long as we took our passports. It must be all right then, we told each other. Nothing could be simpler: there was a regular bus service direct to Vukovar, so we could get there and back in a day. Perfect.

It did seem odd, though, that no one showed the slightest surprise at our wanting to go to a place that was apparently a pile of rubble, with just a fraction of the surviving inhabitants still living among the ruins. The tourist information lady admitted that she had never been to Vukovar, but she was sure there was nothing to worry about...

It all seemed a bit too easy to me, and a nagging thought at the back of my mind was that perhaps the people of Novi Sad did not know what happened in Vukovar. It was entirely possible that the Serbian press had simply reported the 'liberation' of Vukovar without detailing the massive scale of murder and destruction that shocked Western newspaper readers: 'a crime without parallel in post-war Europe'. And even though the place was only an hour's drive away, there was no particular reason why people from Novi Sad should have been there. It seemed hardly credible, but everyone, even the ticket vendor at the bus station, behaved as if there was nothing unusual at all about travelling to this notorious place.

There was something unnatural about all this normality. Almost as soon as we had arrived in Serbia we had noticed it. There was a trade and oil embargo, yet cars sped by at petrol-guzzling speeds. Shops were well stocked, and there was plenty of food everywhere. Of course UN sanctions had only been imposed just over a month ago, and nobody was heating their homes at this time of year. But Serbia was not without resources anyway, producing 20 per cent of its own oil needs and all of its food requirements. Also, as we were to see later, illicit trading of petrol and other goods was rampant along the motorway and Danube. International truck drivers and the captains of river barges were doing a roaring trade.

People were relaxed and going about their business, and nothing on the surface showed us that anyone was under any kind of strain or worry. In the restaurants no one even stopped to listen when radios or televisions broadcast news programmes. Life appeared to be carrying on as usual. So off we went, without a shred of evidence to argue against it.

We expected the journey to take around an hour. Vukovar lies on the main highway connecting Novi Sad with the Croatian city of Osijek, but to our surprise the bus took a tiny country road instead, meandering along the Danube and stopping in countless little villages along the way. It was beautiful, but hardly what we wanted if we were to return the same day. (Later we discovered there was a very good reason for this route: the highway had been abandoned by traffic for months because it had been destroyed by tanks and was now the exclusive domain of the Serbian military. What was officially a 'pacified' area was far from safe.)

It was a hot day and the bus became a stifling sweat box but, at last, we reached the military checkpoint that marked the old borderline between Serbia and the north-east Croatian province of Slavonia. (Not to be confused with the newly independent state of Slovenia, in the north-west of former Yugoslavia.) A handful of soldiers stood by the guard box, machine-guns slung across their chests and pistols hanging off their belts. One spoke with the driver while another passed up the aisle checking documents. We were among the last rows of seats and all went smoothly until our passports appeared.

The soldier stared at my passport for some time, then Benoît's, and then a flick of the fingers told us to follow him.

'Any bags? Bring them too,' he motioned in sign language.

'Just a minute,' I smiled at the bus driver as forty pairs of eyes watched us leave in silence. We were in the middle of nowhere, so I had no intention of being left behind.

A captain frowned as he looked at our passports while his colleague stared over his shoulder. The idling engine gave the interview an urgency, but no one felt it except us, and perhaps the driver. Eventually the captain turned to speak to us in Serbo-Croat and all I could do was give him my best smile and shrug.

'Tourist. *Engelski*,' I said, which did not please him.

The next thing we knew, he had told the bus driver to carry on. We were an unusual catch for this border post and not to be released until he decided.

'Vukovar no,' he motioned with a wagging finger, and that was that:

we had missed the bus and were stranded, not to mention had lost the money on our tickets.

Again he tried to talk with us, but it was impossible since we had no language in common, and all I could do was keep smiling and repeating that we were tourists. My camera bag elicited particular suspicion and after everything had been examined and opened, he managed to convey that I should have a special permit for it from Belgrade. But it was obvious that we had never had any chance of reaching Vukovar and we cursed the officials in Novi Sad. (And what about the article in the British news-paper? Probably a flight of fancy.) The Serbian army was not about to let foreigners see its most notorious feat of destruction on Croatian territory to date.

The sun beat down on the small guard box by the roadside and we stood outside while they held a conference about us. A phone call was made on a radio telephone, and we wondered what on earth was in store for us. Outside, by the road block, stood a huge soldier bristling with arms, who never spoke nor even made eye contact with us. We whiled away the time eyeing the bombed-out farmhouses just past the barrier, where stray dogs and children were playing among the ruins. The roof of the nearest building sagged in the middle, a huge hole marking a direct hit. Its walls were pockmarked from gun fire, and I wondered what had happened to the people who had lived here once. I wished I could take a photo, but that was out of the question. I was lucky my camera was not confiscated altogether.

At last the captain asked me back into his den and I tried not to laugh when it transpired none of them could read our passports. Of course: they could only read Cyrillic script and the writing in our documents was a complete mystery to them. Serbia and Macedonia have an Orthodox Christian tradition and thus their writing is in Cyrillic, the same as in Russia. I enjoyed my little shred of power as I pointed out what our names were, our places of birth, etc.

A policeman arrived from the nearest town on the Serbian side and yet another conference was held. The soldiers had been reserved but not unfriendly. This man was quite different. He was the kind who relishes the authority of his position and the first thing he wanted was to see the contents of our pockets. If he had wanted to body search us I would not have been surprised, but thankfully he did not go that far. Instead he took our passports and, after keeping us waiting a while longer, motioned us to get into his car. He was going to take us back to the nearest town and bus station where we could return to Novi Sad – at least that was what the captain implied.

Instead, however, we found ourselves driven at breakneck speed to the nearest police station, where the whole rigmarole began again, this time in a warren of corridors and rooms full of beady-eyed policemen. Benoît was pushed out of the reception room with a jab to his chest and we both stood in an unlit corridor, wondering what on earth was going to happen. Benoît was seething by this time, ready to start shouting, and I tried hard to calm him. Getting angry was pointless. But it was an unnerving feeling, being stuck in a police station, denuded of our passports and no idea if we would ever get them back. I silently worried that we might be deported. Packs of uniformed men moved past us from time to time, but they never included our interrogator, and nobody else took any notice of us. We were in limbo.

Luckily it turned out the policeman was just keeping us hanging around for his own fun, but since we could not communicate, he soon got bored and let us go. Passports safely in our pockets, we stepped out into the afternoon sunshine and breathed easier at last. We were free to return to Novi Sad and we set off to find the bus station.

The town was called Šid (pronounced 'Shid'), which was close enough to what we thought of the place. It was a horizontal town of squat, concrete houses and grubby streets. Soldiers were everywhere and the atmosphere was distinctly macho. No women seemed to walk alone, and the handful of restaurants and bars were full of drunk men playing cards, revolvers stuck between bulging guts and trouser belts or casually sticking out of back pockets. The sooner we could leave the better, only the next bus was not for another two hours, so we hung about the least-exposed snack bar we could find, and tried not to draw attention to ourselves.

It was a long time before we were back in the tranquil setting of Sremska Kamenica, returned from a project that had been futile from the start – if only we had known it. But at least we had come to no harm and had the satisfaction of having found out what no one in Novi Sad seemed to know: that visiting Vukovar was not that simple if you were a foreigner.

We settled on our balcony with a bottle of wine and some local sausage, and the day's tensions and disappointment faded quickly. The scene around us was enough to raise our spirits, for not only was there the view of the sweeping Danube and setting sun, but also the goings-on outside the house.

Beneath our balcony was the verandah, overgrown by shading ivy, where long tables and benches had been creaking under the weight of a party ever since our arrival the day before. Musicians played and sang there for hours on end, and we enjoyed listening to their lively music. An accordion and a couple of fiddles accompanied the male voices, sometimes melancholy and slow, rising to emotional crescendos; other times full of energy and ever faster, fiddles speeding up the refrain with every breath. It was the kind of singing you could imagine Cossacks dancing to, legs shooting from the hip, knee-high from the ground. The rhythms recalled the ancient rush of mounted warriors, the stamping feet of grooms circling the swirling skirts of crisp-cottoned brides, or the sad cries of a widowed mother. It was as emotional as the Moravian songs we had heard in Strážnice – only with a much stronger undertone of violence.

Each evening, as the hours wore on, the singing and talking got louder, glasses were smashed and, eventually, drunken bodies lurched to their cars, restrained by friends but inevitably let go when knives were drawn. It was a chaotic, raucous celebration that was going on downstairs, but we never saw the participants in daylight. Each morning all was peace and tranquillity, and the breakfast included in our bill was never served. In fact, we could easily have left without paying and nobody would have noticed. Clearly our custom was of no importance to this 'hotel', and we discovered later that the proprietor was the local Mafia boss, recently returned from making his fortune in Germany. The house was brand new, and we were the first guests of his legitimate business.

After the frustrations of the day before, we decided to treat ourselves to a third day in Novi Sad, spending a leisurely morning exploring the environs of Petrovaradin fortress and browsing in the town for maps. The fortress was built up to its present proportions by the Austrians, intent on keeping the Turks at bay after they had besieged Vienna, in 1683, and it took over one hundred years and countless lives to complete it. You can believe it too as you ascend the immense drive and pass under successive gates, overgrown with weeds now, but still intact. The view from its ramparts is beautiful. Across the Danube, Novi Sad forms a hybrid shape of old and new architecture, the Vojvodina plain stretching out into the dusty distance, while all around the fortress rise the wooded hills of the Fruška Gora range, where ancient monasteries hide.

Later, while searching for a good map, we stumbled across a friendly bookstore behind the cathedral. It was run by a couple of young men with tousled hair and intense expressions – the kind you can meet on any university campus around the world.

'Where are you from?' asked one of them. 'England? Oh, I love England! But what are you doing here?'

'Well, we're travelling through Eastern Europe and Serbia, to see what is going on for ourselves ... Can you tell me what is going on with this country?'

'What's going on? Nobody knows what's going on,' he replied smiling. 'Of course nobody listens to the radio or the newspapers! It's all propaganda. How are we supposed to know anything?' he asked with a shrug. 'You tried to go to Vukovar?' Are you mad!' he asked to astounded looks, and we all laughed.

'Yes but, you see, we wanted to see what a bombed-out city looks like.'

They shook their heads. 'These English! They're mad.'

Only one of the three men around us could speak English, but the other two were determined to join the conversation, so Alexander – as our new friend was called – got caught in a volley of questions and answers he could hardly translate fast enough for our eager sentences. We formed an electric little bunch in a corner of the shop, very soon buzzing with theories and ideas about the war.

One of the men was a darkly brooding person, piercing me with searching eyes that had a hunted look about them. The barrier of language was almost intolerable for him and he shot his sentences at Alexander in hurried whispers. He was an ardent Marxist, still, and his views were extreme, even for his friends. But Alexander loyally translated for him, with only the occasional caveat that these were not his own opinions. According to his friend, however, the root of this war had to do with the fact that the Serb president, Slobodan Milošević, is a traitor who worked for the CIA in the sixties and is now leading his people into war at the behest of the US, who cannot tolerate a Moslem state in Europe. It seemed like Cold War paranoia to us, but we did meet a few others who shared this view.

Alexander, on the other hand, had a more spiritual attitude. He argued that communism made Yugoslavs morally corrupt and spiritually sick, and that the war is an expression of that sickness, of a sick people. For him communism was a blueprint for destroying the soul and, by extension, society. Worst of all, communism destroyed religious values, so people have nothing to fall back on at this time. Whole generations have been perverted.

The psychological damage of a system based on intense indoctrination and fear paralysed the mind and has left people unable to think for themselves and therefore easily led by power-crazed individuals like Milošević. Independent thinking and decision-making has been discouraged for so long, people do not have the courage to distinguish between right and wrong and stand by their views, even if in their hearts they know the difference. That is why old communists like Milošević have been able to stay in power. People prefer to follow a strong leader, who will give them a cause to follow: in this case nationalism.

He spoke persuasively and sensitively, and was a perfect example that not all Serbs are monsters, as portrayed in the Western press.

'I am a Serb,' he said, 'but I am first and foremost Alexander, an individual. I cannot be responsible for this war and I am not guilty for being a Serb.'

I knew just how he felt. How often had I said similar things all that time ago, at school?

'But what can be done?' I asked. 'Is there no opposition movement at all?'

'Yes, there is, but it is still weak. There were demonstrations in Belgrade a month or so ago. But the momentum was lost and people are still too scared to openly come out against the authorities. We are not enough people, because the majority of ordinary workers and rural folk support Milošević. They think he is what's needed to make Serbia great again and avenge the suffering of the last World War. They have bitter memories, and you have to remember that this is a country with a tradition of blood feuds. Living by the gun is a vital part of our culture.'

Speaking of which, it seemed odd that these healthy young men were not in the army. Every male over the age of eighteen was supposed to be on stand-by. All three of them were evading the authorities, they said, keeping a low profile and trying to avoid the nightmare as long as possible.

'If I think they're about to get me, I'll move into a remote part of the countryside,' was Alexander's answer to the problem. But it was obvious that all of them lived in fear of what might happen. None wanted to take any part in this war and I felt uselessly sorry for them.

Like most other nationals of the former Eastern Bloc, their passports do not gain them entry to many Western countries these days, and there was nowhere to run to. There was no point heading anywhere else in Eastern Europe and, anyway, they had no money to go far. There was bitterness in Alexander's voice when he spoke of his last experience of trying to visit England, a place he had once spent a happy year in. He had been arrested at Heathrow airport, thrown into a cell and treated like a common criminal before being deported back to Belgrade. Before he was dispatched, the British authorities stamped his passport, making him out as officially undesirable, blocking him from marking future visits, and his last memory of England is being frog-marched to a departing plane.

Alexander and his friends are trapped in their own country. All they can do is watch events with increasing horror and resentment at the West for taking sides in a war without any acceptable justification for any side.

BELGRADE

Our arrival in Belgrade was like your worst Kafka nightmare. What looked like a fine, cosmopolitan city at first glance turned out to be full of mind-bending contradictions and dead-ends. A place where friendly advice led nowhere at all and words belied reality.

Yet when we reached the city, we were impressed with what we saw: stacked high above the confluence of the rivers Danube and Sava, the great fortress of Kalemegdan spearheads a densely packed throng of oriental domes and church spires among domino lines of apartment blocks, squeezed tight by cool high-rise buildings and massive civic palaces. Bridges as long as any crossing the Hudson River to Manhattan serve the approaches from the north, and we had plenty of time to enjoy the view and wonder what life might be like under that exciting skyline. Everything I had read about Belgrade spoke of a drab city, with little to keep the visitor, but that was far from the impression the city made on us, an impression we never lost.

Luckily we came into the city at just the right place to find the central tourist office, and Benoît made enquiries for somewhere to stay. But prices were incredible compared to what we had been paying, and seemed quite unreasonable considering there were no customers. Even the youth hostel was charging US$15 per person, so the lady directed us to the most central campsite instead.

But cycling there was like getting trapped inside an Escher drawing, where there is no escape and you keep finding yourself back where you started. The city is spread over countless hills and its streets sweep up interminable inclines, which certainly make for interesting views, but do little for the cyclist.

Around two million people live here, so orientation is not that easy,

especially if you cannot read in Cyrillic. All the street signs were exclusively written in the Orthodox hand, but on our map they were in Latin
writing. I tried desperately to remember my handful of Russian lessons
from months ago, but could only remember about five letters, and we
were reduced to trying to match the layout of the map to the streets we
were on. Soon we were hopelessly lost.

After climbing one particularly long hill, we had the bright idea of
checking the tram numbers against the map and, sure enough, we were
going the wrong way. We debated whether to cut across or retrace our
route, and reluctantly decided it was probably safer to return the way we
had come. At least that way we had one fixed point to work from, and we
enjoyed a brief respite sailing downhill.

Our landmark was a large roundabout, and a friendly man helped us
decipher the words on our map.

'This is *Revolucije* street, and then *pravo*, straight ahead.'

'Thank you very much,' we said.

'No problem.'

'No problem' seemed to be a favourite phrase in this country, but it
already had a hollow ring to it for us.

Almost all the roads leading off the roundabout were uphill and of
course the one we had to take was one of them. It was not long, however
before we realised there must be some mistake. We could not read the
street signs, but we could clearly see a large stadium marked on the map,
which we now seemed to be passing, but which we should not, if we were
on the right road.

This time I decided we would try and cut across, the thought of
descending yet again too tedious, and again we got lost in the maze of
hills. There were few people about to ask directions in this neighbourhood, but eventually we saw a man standing outside a villa. He was
clearly a guard, for the building was draped in red flags depicting heroic
soldiers, and he had a gun at his side.

'Do you speak English?' I asked, as he eyed us suspiciously, walkie-
talkie at the ready. No he did not. But a secretary inside did, and she
efficiently drew us a small map with the street names in Latin and Cyrillic,
so we could recognise them. The campsite was not far away, she assured
us, and we thanked her gratefully.

'What is this place?' I asked on leaving, and she replied it was the central headquarters for volunteers for the Serbian militia. How typical of us to stumble across such a place ...

Months later I recognised the villa in a television report and it was not so much the headquarters for the State militia as the home of the most notorious Serbian paramilitary group, known as The Tigers and lead by Zeljko Ražnjatović, otherwise called Arkan, the butcher of Vukovar. No wonder the guard had seemed unduly paranoid. This was not a place that wanted foreign visitors.

It was Arkan's forces that perpetrated – still are perpetrating – the most disgusting murders of helpless civilians, and he is listed as a war criminal by the United Nations, not to mention wanted by Interpol for crimes ranging from murder to bank robbery in various European countries. He is a professional criminal for whom the war is his greatest bounty yet, and his personal fortune through looting Croatian and Bosnian homes is said to be inestimable.

In spite of international condemnation his power and influence in Serbia is undisputed and, in the elections of December 1992, he even gained respectability by becoming the elected member of parliament for the province of Kosovo. Standing for the ultra-nationalist Radical Party, his election bodes ill for the Moslem Albanian majority in that province. If the war ever spreads to that region Arkan's men are guaranteed to lead the slaughter. Yet hidden in a leafy suburb of Belgrade, the Tigers' head-quarters looks totally innocuous and you could never imagine that the pretty secretary who helped us there could have anything to do with murdering thugs.

She sent us on our way with a friendly smile and once more we set off. First it was up and then it was down, and eventually we found ourselves in a forest covering yet another hill, pushing the bikes up a lumpy path and wondering if we would ever get there. We passed a cemetery and later a large pack of stray dogs, and the atmosphere became distinctly ominous. At last we saw a sign for camping, but my heart sank as soon as I saw a row of camouflaged tents. The site had been taken over by the military and a gruff man told us there was no question of staying there. It had taken two hours to find this blasted place!

Why did the tourist office not know that the campsite had been requisitioned? Why had the regular soldiers we had lastly asked for directions said nothing? Our tired minds failed miserably to make sense of it all. Hot, sweaty and exhausted, we had to accept the fact that we had wasted our time and that we could not stay. All we could do was refill our water-bottles and leave, taunted by the sight of the distant Danube and Novi Beograd on the other side of the river, where another campsite was supposed to be. It was almost exactly at the point where we had arrived, many hours ago.

'Down the hill and turn right,' the man had said, but we lost the trail within the first five minutes. 'Left and right and left and right,' said another man, and the first wrong turn led us inexplicably on to a concrete flyover for trams.

'Benoît we're going the wrong way!' I cried. 'Benoît! Stop!'

'I know we're going the wrong way, what d'you want me to do about it?' he snapped.

That we should not be there was obvious, but it was too late to turn back so we simply carried on, even while an angry tram rang its bell coming the other way. It was absurd, but we began to feel haunted, as if the city had some kind of malevolent power that made it impossible to get out.

The sun was beginning to set and still we were far from rest. The tourist office was closed by now and the hotels were well beyond our means. There was no alternative but to look for the other campsite. At least the Danube could not be missed, and we crossed over to the northern suburbs, into a tangle of spaghetti junctions and motorway entrances, where we wasted yet more time trying to find the right exit. There were even less pedestrians near these fast roads, but thankfully another cyclist stopped to show us the way, and we cycled in the darkening light, buffeted by speeding traffic as we headed along a motorway. The campsite was supposed to be attached to the first motel stop.

We found the site, but it was closed due to lack of tourists, and no amount of pleading would persuade the concierge to let us stay. He was a fat toad of a man whose chin melted into a pile of flab beneath his face and his attitude was one of total indifference. He never even raised his eyes to look at me while he was speaking. Defeated I asked what he was charging for a room in the motel. 'One hundred Deutschmarks,' he replied, and I turned on my heels.

We pushed our bikes along the perimeter fence of the empty campsite and gazed exhausted at the wash-house. What to do? It was pointless returning to the city. If even this dump was charging so much, what could the city's hotels be charging? We debated our plight with a car trader, who had his lot here, and he kindly put in a word for us with the toad. But it was no good, he would not budge and I'm afraid I used my last weapon, which came quite naturally by this stage: I cried. The weary hours of pointless effort had brought me to the end of my tether and I let myself go in helpless abandon. We had cycled approximately 90 kilometres so far and I could take no more.

The car trader stared at us uncomfortably while Benoît tried to comfort me, and eventually he was prompted to make one last attempt to help us. What does it look like treating foreigners like this? he asked the manager on the phone. These people have come to visit our country and they should not be treated with such disregard. What does it look like for Serbia? This was excellent talk, and brought the desired result at last. We could stay. Not for free, of course, but for an outrageous US$16.

No matter. We had found a safe resting place, and the fact that there was no hot water or electricity was neither here no there. The tent was up in no time at all, a meal prepared in expert time, and we sat in the dark, eating soup with a bottle of wine Benoît had been thoughtful enough to buy earlier on. It was small comfort, but extremely welcome, and we marvelled at how quickly our fortunes could change on this journey. The night before we had been sleeping in the lap of luxury, surrounded by beautiful views. Tonight we were sitting in the dark by a motorway junction for twice the price.

Belgrade was no place for us to stay and next morning we made straight for the nearest town along the Danube. It was a small place called Smederevo, 40 kilometres east of the capital, which we found without too much difficulty, and only the gorgeous landscape of undulating hills slowed down our progress. We sweated and puffed over a roller-coaster road, past fragrant peach orchards and buzzing villages, past verdant fields and occasional forest, and the red-tiled roofs of whitewashed houses.

Even panting up hills we could not fail to notice the beauty all around us and we stopped often to enjoy the views and eat fresh peaches sold along the roadside. The summer heat was intense, but that only height-ened the rich scents of ripening fruit and drying hay, and every breath was delicious.

It was hard to imagine that a country so lovely could harbour such violent passions as were fuelling the war, just a few hours drive to the west. The sense of security that breathed from this fertile land contradicted all ideas of violence, and I tried to fathom the shock that must be engulfing farmers, whose homes and lives are being destroyed – not by nature but by human nature, which it is impossible to understand or predict.

I tried to picture what the villages around us would look like with their windows blown out and roofs shattered, but the leap of imagination was too great. Yet the army of Serb fighters is creating just such a picture in the name of these peaceful villages here, and I wondered to what extent they really knew it. Even so close to the capital, the politicians and their armies must seem far away from rural concerns. But I was forgetting the ancient history of violence in this country, and it has always been the rural population that has borne the brunt of the fighting and killing.

People have very long memories here, and the deaths and crimes of the last war are not forgotten. Perhaps revenge is sweet for the Serbian farmers right now. An estimated 200,000–700,000 people – most of them Serbs – died in the Jasenovac death camp alone, run by the Nazi puppet state of Croatia during the Second World War. (Jasenovac is located at the confluence of the rivers Una and Sava, on the northern border between Croatia and Bosnia, and was the largest of several concentration camps.) Another 10,000 were slaughtered by unspeakable torture in the Kozara mountains of northern Bosnia, including large numbers of children, and the list goes on. (Robert Fisk, for *The Independent*, put the total number of people killed in the Kozara campaign as high as 66,000, of which 11,000 were children.) Many hundreds of thousands more died in the civil war that broke out between the Resistance fighters after 1941, when Croat-led partisans fought anti-communist, mostly Serb, Chetniks.

Let no one believe that the State of Yugoslavia was created by anything other than the suppression of all national and political rights, be they Serbian, Croatian, Moslem or Macedonian – to mention just a few. It was the iron grip of communism under Marshal Tito (a Croat) that held the country together, and its peace was a false one, apparently going against human nature. If there had been freedom to protest and fight for self-determination, it would have happened a long time ago, just as it would have done in the former Soviet Union.

★

In Smederevo we found a peaceful haven in a small guest house set back from the road, where delicious meals of *ćevapčići* and home-made bread were served on a cool terrace. The bread was soft and thick, almost like an Indian nan, ideal for soaking up the juicy sauce of the minced-meat rolls that became our favourite dish and, as always, we drank the wonderful *Banatski* wine to go with it, relished all the more for costing no more than a dollar per litre.

Later I discovered that this wine had an unexpected German connection, coming as it does from the Banat, a historic region outlined by the Danube and Maros rivers to the south and north, the Hungarian Tisza River to the west and the Transylvanian Alps of Romania to the east. It is a compact area once ruled entirely by Hungary, and it is from that time that it derives its name, 'Ban' originally meaning 'provincial governor' in Hungarian.

Today most of the Banat lies in Romanian territory, with only a narrow slither in Hungary and Serbia. But for almost two hundred years, from the fifteenth to eighteenth century, it was under Turkish rule and, like the Hungarian plain, became severely depopulated. Only after the Habsburg armies had pushed the Ottomans south of the Danube was the Banat repopulated, and the policy of both Maria Theresa and Joseph II was to colonise the area with Germans, who they thought would work hardest at turning marshland into good farming country.

Hundreds of boats came down the Danube from towns like Ulm, bringing young peasants from Swabia, the Palatinate and Rhineland, who were to settle here and bring renewed prosperity. Naturally they brought their traditional skills with them too, and since many of them came from famous wine-growing regions in Germany, it is not surprising that their wine is good, even today after almost all Germans have been expelled or have joined the exodus that began after 1945 and accelerated drastically after 1989.

They paid the price of their origins for wars and crimes that were not their own, the policy of revenge ensuring that many thousands were deported to Russian labour camps, their land expropriated, or their families expelled to a homeland they no longer knew. Many Banat Germans found the modern culture of West Germany completely alien, and depression and suicide are not uncommon among them. They are products of a bygone age, even their language marking them out as strange remnants of a forgotten past. Many do not even speak German, having assimilated to Hungarian or Romanian culture and language generations ago. No one would know they had ever existed if it were not for their books and memoirs still being published in German today.

Like its originators, there is nothing fancy about *Banatski* wine. It is simply a refreshing, dry white wine that is excellent with good country food, and it was while sitting on the terrace, enjoying yet another bottle, that we got talking to Smetijlana. Her daughter had heard us speaking English, and soon they were both sitting at our table, eager to practise.

Smetijlana was a lively woman of thirty-seven, with a quick wit and an easy smile. Her English was excellent and, as soon as she told us she was from Bosnia, we got talking about the war. In fact, she and her daughter were refugees, having left their Serbian village in Bosnia fearing for their safety. Her husband was left behind, and every day she was wondering how he was coping alone, hiding in their flat. It had been too risky for him to travel with them because, as a man, he was liable to be forced into military service by the first checkpoint they were stopped at. There had been no choice but to leave him behind, at the mercy of help from other villagers because he had lost his job and had no means of support.

Smetijlana's money was soon going to run out too. But at least she could go to Belgrade, where the refugee office for displaced Serbs was giving out emergency funds for housing and upkeep. (According to the Foreign Minister of Federal Yugoslavia, 600,000 refugees were in Serbia and Montenegro in February 1993, with more expected.)

The authorities were using many empty hotels and campsites to put up Serbian refugees from Croatia and Bosnia, and that, along with military requisitions, was to make finding somewhere to stay difficult throughout our time in Serbia. Either we could not stay, or the price was astronomical because the management was trying to make up lost revenue. It was hardly a problem, however, because we were lucky enough to meet kind and generous people, who gave us hospitality in their homes. In fact, they positively urged us to stay with them.

'It is ridiculous, you know,' said Smetijlana, 'Moslems are Serbs too! My village in Bosnia was a mixed village of Serbs and Moslems, even Croats, and we all lived together just fine until this. There are many mixed marriages and we could have carried on living together without this war.'

'But what is this war really about?' I asked, eager for her point of view.

'You have to understand that it was Serbs who made Yugoslavia possible in the first place. They fought and died for this country to be established. Half a million people died in the First World War here. Two million people died in the Second World War, that was 10 per cent of the population, and the majority were Serbs. Can you understand that after all that, Serbs, who are the largest group of people in Yugoslavia, could not allow the Federation to break up, and least of all let themselves be treated as a minority in their own country? It is deeply insulting.

'What happened in Croatia after their government declared independence in June last year [1991] made life impossible for Serbs. First of all: they were now treated like a minority, and Croat was declared the official language, which also meant abolishing the Cyrillic script, since Croats are Roman Catholic and use Latin writing. But, worst of all: all Serbs were asked to sign a document of loyalty to the Croatian State, and if they did not, they were sacked from their jobs.

'Can you imagine their feelings? Losing their jobs was just the first step to persecution. The majority of civil servants in Croatia, working in government offices, with the police and army, were Serbs. Now they were suddenly not good enough. What was the next step going to be?

'The new Croatian government is a reincarnation of the fascist Ustasha regime, and they are bound to do the same as they did during the last war, when they built extermination camps for Serbs, worse than the Nazis.'

My head was reeling from this battery of arguments, but I had to keep listening. It was too important. The words came tumbling out in a highly articulate stream and all I could do was try to keep up.

'You see, the Croats have the support of the Germans once more. Who was it that pushed for acceptance of the new, independent Croatia? The Germans. They want control of the Adriatic coast so they are helping the Croats with arms and food.'

This was a suggestion I had not heard before. After all, Germany hardly needs to control the Yugoslav Adriatic politically for economic benefit. Half the land and tourist industry there is probably German-owned anyway. Istria and Dalmatia is to Germans what the Spanish Costa del Sol is to the British. However, the comment showed that deep-seated mistrust has survived nearly fifty years of increasingly good relations between Germany and Yugoslavia prior to this conflict. (Doubtless many

Europeans mistrust Germany on principle. But I have also heard what Spanish people have to say about the British invasion of Andalucía and it is rarely flattering.)

'I still believe war could have been avoided,' sighed our friend, 'but once the killing started there could be no living together any more. Once a brother or a mother had been killed, there was no forgiving and forgetting.'

'So what could be the solution?' we asked. The answer was emphatic.

'Separation. It is the only way forward now. There is too much hatred. Each group must live in separate territory. I don't care if the Moslems want to live under Islamic law, but they cannot force me into it. If that means moving somewhere else, so be it, but we must be allowed to live with our own kind, with our own laws and customs.'

It was the answer we were to hear wherever we went.

The Western press has portrayed Serbia as the aggressor, bandied about charged words like 'ethnic cleansing' and 'Greater Serbia'. But what it has failed to explore is the historic background and genuine fears that have made ordinary, decent people believe that they are fighting for their very existence. Slobodan Milošević may be a cynical manipulator only interested in power, but the forces he has unleashed have been galvanised by deep-seated fears he has successfully reawakened in the majority of Serbs. (It is the same spark that could ignite Hungary or Slovakia as well.)

Perhaps if Western politicians had been less criminally ignorant of Yugoslav history, they would not have recognised Croatia so quickly, a prerequisite for almost certain war with Serbia, given the local conditions. The arrogance of Western solutions for other people's problems, which they have not taken the time to fully understand, has yet again led to an open sore of violence that now seems as impossible to heal as the war between the Palestinians and Israelis. The West has the blood of these wars on its hands too.

Hitch-hiking or catching a bus into Belgrade was easy from Smederevo and, now that we had a cheap and pleasant base, we could discover what was behind the city's promising façade. By now I had put the amber theme of our journey to the back of my mind, and my attention was firmly fixed on the present: not only did I want to explore the capital, but I also wanted to make contact with Serbian PEN. If its members were as helpful as those in Budapest, more interesting encounters were bound to result.

But on our first day we simply went to meet the city, walking about its busy centre, where Kneza Mihailova makes up the central shopping avenue. Closed to traffic, it is also the main busking stage, and itinerant musicians mixed with begging Gypsies and pavement vendors. Animated clusters of arguing men stood by corners, ice-cream sellers sold delicious cones of freshly crushed fruit and ice, and we wandered among them like happy tourists. 'Deutschmarks, Deutschmarks, dollar, dollar,' whispered the money-changers in our ears, waving huge wads of unwanted Serbian dinars. But we just laughed and passed by, the lesson of Gdańsk not forgotten.

In the early evening people turned out for their daily stroll – called a *korso* here – and Belgrade at dusk was as vibrant as any south European city could be: full of whole families on their evening promenade.

Only the long tables selling political propaganda and nationalist music betrayed the serious times people were living in. Posters picturing heroes of the Serbian Resistance during the Second World War plastered every placard. Badges, flags and banners were for sale, not to mention gruesome booklets purporting to show Croat atrocities during the last war as well as the present. But not too many people were crowding to buy these gory wares, and many even seemed to be giving them a wide berth. The average pedestrian no more wanted to see pictures of mutilated bodies than English shoppers like to stop at anti-vivisection stalls.

If you followed Mihailova avenue to its end, you came out at the edge of the Kalemegdan fortifications, where a leafy park covered the outer ramparts. There were several levels of buttressed earth, with immense walls securing a multitude of stone gates and tunnels, until at last you reached the inner sanctum, where a breezy plateau looked out over the strategic confluence of two mighty rivers: the Danube and the Sava.

For centuries these two rivers marked the border between the Ottoman and Habsburg Empires, between East and West, Islam and Christianity. As recently as 1867, this fortress was Turkish-held, and the intrepid Mary Edith Durham, travelling here in 1904, met plenty of people who still remembered the brutal janissaries, who terrorised them. The worst of it was that these janissaries were their own flesh and blood, privileged guardians of Turkish rule, who had been taken from Serbian families as children, converted to Islam, and been specially trained to police the local population.

Today the Sava River marks a long section of the northern border between Croatia and Bosnia-Hercegovina, only splitting away from that line north-west of the town of Banja Luka, where the border curves in an irregular path, first south and then south-east, along the Adriatic coast. It gives Croatia a very odd shape, but what is significant about it in relation to the present war is that most of this border follows the old Austro-Hungarian defences, which were manned predominantly by Serbs.

It was the policy of the Habsburgs to grant refuge – even to encourage immigration – to Serbs fleeing from Turkish-occupied lands in the south-east during the sixteenth, seventeenth and eighteenth centuries. (Therein lies the reason why Albanians make up around 90 per cent of the population in the Serbian province of Kosovo. The original inhabitants fled before the Turkish armies, leaving the territory to Albanian settlers.)

Tens of thousands of Serbian families settled along this Habsburg version of the Roman *limes* – known locally as the *Vojna Krajina* – and were given protection and privileges in return for a lifetime of being on military stand-by. It is for this reason that Serbian communities are now found in the much-fought-over Krajina region of modern Croatia and Bosnia. They are the descendants of Serbian soldiers who have lived here for several centuries and, naturally enough, now consider these regions their homeland, even though Serbia proper is much further to the east.

This policy of resettlement also contributed to a historic tension between these Serbian communities and their Croat and Bosnian neighbours. For not only were they settled over the heads of the local Croatian and Hungarian nobility, but they were also exempt from their authority and right to demand taxes. So not only the authorities resented them, but the local population as well, who had to pay dues to their local lords as well as the Habsburg rulers. The settlers were further marked out as alien by the fact that they adhered to the Serbian Orthodox Church, while Croatians belonged to the Roman Catholic Church, which has acted as a lasting social wedge to this day.

Thus the Serbian communities living in the remote, mountainous regions of the Krajina evolved with a highly defensive tradition, both mentally and practically. Their sense of identity is deeply rooted in their uniquely autonomous tradition and they will defend it to the last, irrespective of what any outsiders tell them.

This was the basis for the Serb militants of the region demanding an independent 'Republic of Serbian Krajina' in Croatian territory. They were thinking in strictly narrow-minded, local terms. The fact that they played into the hands of Slobodan Milošević is, of course, quite another matter. It is unlikely, however, that the war originates in a master plan for a Serbian Empire. Rather, events have conspired to make it appear that way to those who wish to promote that interpretation of the war. It is hardly that simple.

When the Western press uses these militants to underline the argument that Serbia is trying to establish a 'Greater Serbian Empire' they are being disingenuous if they do not explain the presence of Serbs in the Krajina region. Whatever their political opinion may be, it is only natural for them not to want to leave the homes and villages they have lived in for generations, just as it is natural for them not to want to be ruled by the dictates of Zagreb, or Belgrade for that matter.

Reading the Western press coverage of the war, one would never guess that there was a shred of reason on the Serbian side; all righteousness it seems is with the Croatians and Bosnians. This is not so, and even the UN troops, who have witnessed the fighting for themselves, admit that no side is innocent of unspeakable atrocities. All are guilty. And yet it is important to remember that an entire people cannot be defined by the acts of either their political leaders or those who kill in their name.

An old Jewish man from Sarajevo, interviewed by a *Guardian* reporter in June 1992, made a very important point: 'They try to say that what is going on here is a war between Serbs and Moslems and Croats, but it is not true. It is a war between terrorist killers and ordinary people.'

I regret that we never met any Croats or Moslems who could tell us their side of the story. However, it has been given ample coverage elsewhere and, in the end, there is no justice or redeeming argument for what has happened. The third Balkan war this century is a man-made disaster, like all the others.

NADIR

Wer weit gereist, wird oftmals Dinge schauen,
Sehr fern von dem, was er für Wahrheit hielt.
(Who travels far and wide, will often make discoveries
that challenge the truth once cherished.)[1]

Hermann Hesse, *Die Morgenlandfahrt*, 1959

My welcome at Serbian PEN was rather like our arrival in the country. Apparently I was the first foreign writer to visit them since the war had started. No journalists had been here either, no doubt preferring the excitement and opportunities of Sarajevo, from where their stories were more likely to get published, and I was told that even overseas writers' organisations had started returning invitations and publications unanswered. Yet I found it hard to believe that no one had come to what had to be an excellent source for Serbian opinions.

'Meet Natascha,' said Predrag, 'she has come to hear our points of view for herself,' and I was ushered into a lounge of comfy leather sofas. Coffee was ordered and people going about their business were interrupted, invited to come and join us.

The fact that I was neither important nor well connected did not seem to make the slightest difference, my unexpected appearance alone turning me into a special guest. Once again I felt like an impostor — after all, I could do nothing for them, and I was not even sure that I wanted to if I could. I simply wanted to know more to help my own understanding, but that was good enough for Predrag, and soon I was inundated with pamphlets and papers, opinions and counter-claims.

My host was a middle-aged man with a Lenin beard and a manic look. When I first entered his office, he was making phone calls on two

[1] Author's own translation.

156

different phones, checking papers and writing notes, as if against the clock. His brow was covered in tiny beads of sweat, and he seemed to be in another world – oblivious to the presence of others in the room. His head was obviously crammed full of vital matters that he was trying to pursue all at the same time and, even once he was sitting in the lounge, it was hard to keep his attention for more than a few moments. He jumped from one issue to the next with breathtaking speed – whether you had asked to hear about it or not – and I felt in the aura of someone extreme.

Predrag was a man with a mission and I was his perfect subject. I had done nothing more than to ask his opinion, yet I was immediately co-opted into his faith, treated like an acolyte before I even knew what for. It was very quickly apparent, however, that he saw Serbia as the tragic hero in the war against the Croats. (The Moslems somehow did not feature.)

'Do you know about the genocide perpetrated against Serbs in the Second World War? It was not just the Jews that were systematically exterminated, yet the crimes against us have always been ignored, suppressed by Tito and the Vatican.'

He showed me a booklet recently published by the 'Serbian National Defense Council of America', based in Chicago, full of the most repulsive images of torture and killings. Smiling Croatian Ustasha soldiers held up the heads of decapitated prisoners, guts swelled out of slit abdomens, mutilated women and children ... it was no different to the records of Auschwitz – or Bosnia today.

The booklet begins with a gruesome quote attributed to the head of the Nazi puppet state of Croatia, Ante Pavelić, in which he proudly displays forty pounds of human eyes on his desk, gouged out of the heads of Serbs, Jews and Gypsies held in his concentration camps. It goes on to outline the emergence of the Croatian fascists who, with the help of Mussolini and Hitler, eventually became the leaders of the first independent State of Croatia (1941–45). It claims 750,000 Serbs, 60,000 Jews and 26,000 Gypsies were killed in a planned genocide in Croatia that matched the barbarity of the Nazi killing machine.

This State was not only supported by the Axis powers either, but by Pope Pius XII and the Catholic Church in Rome who, according to this booklet, supported the Catholic Croats against the Orthodox Serbs and other religious groups, and it is recorded how Catholic priests took an active part in the betrayal and slaughter of their parishioners; people such as the Franciscan monk Miroslav Filipovič. It claims 158 Orthodox Serbian priests were murdered, and the record of depravity goes on for over thirty pages. One example of many is the description of how it was common practice to load rafts with the heads of children, and set them on the Sava River marked 'Meat for the market of Belgrade'.

Another leaflet, published by the extreme nationalist Association of University Professors and Scientists of Serbia, claims that in October 1991, 'forty bodies of murdered Serbs were found on the banks of the Danube, in the area of the communes of Bac, Bačka Palanka, Novi Sad and Indija.' They report these bodies and others have been found with signs of torture.

To what extent this propaganda is based on truth or half-truth I am in no position to judge. But more sober sources, such as the BBC correspondent, Misha Glenny, have written about the inescapable link in many Serbians' minds between the atrocities committed by the first independent Croatia and the present regime of the Republic of Croatia. The fact that President Tudjman did nothing to allay these fears after independence was declared, instead whipping up existing paranoia by his insensitive policies, did much to pave the way for war.

That once more both Germany and the Vatican have openly sided with Croatia has fanned the flames even further, and it is almost impossible to convince ordinary Serbs that there is no conspiracy to exterminate them. They see the war in terms of survival for their people and their religious faith, and there is no more powerful inspiration for battle than that.

Condemned by the Western press, isolated by UN sanctions, it is easy to see the tragic hero of Serbia growing in people's minds. They supported the Allies during the Second World War, yet now those same countries have deserted them. Thus the academics' leaflet ends in highly emotive language: 'Once again, the Serbian people, all alone this time, has found itself in front of the German mega-empire throwing its shadow across Europe, but first of all, across Serbia.'

There was no point responding to this barrage of information, and Predrag did not require it. I did try to steer the conversation to more recent history, however, interested in his views on the subject of Yugoslavia under Tito. Was there nothing to praise about a ruler – even a communist ruler – who managed to bring such an incompatible population to live as one nation? But this led to another branch of the conspiracy theory, which ran along the lines that Tito, a Croat, had always hated the Serbs, since the time of the Resistance. Therefore his nation-building was developed with the long-term goal of destroying Serbia, or at least weakening the country beyond recovery.

According to Predrag, the only way the Serbian majority within the Yugoslav nation could be contained was by devising a system of federal republics, each with the power to run its internal affairs, so that rightful Serbian dominion was made impossible. The reforms of the 1974 Constitution were a milestone in this programme, which was also when Moslems were given nation status. By creating these autonomous republics within the Yugoslav system, Tito paved the way for independent republics in the future. It was, so to speak a blueprint for a second Croatian Republic, should communist Yugoslavia ever break up after his death. (Tito died in 1980.) This is patently absurd, since it is inconceivable that a committed communist leader, such as Tito, would ever have planned for the eventuality of his system failing – especially not in the 1970s, before Gorbachov.

It was mind-boggling to be drawn into the paranoid world of Predrag's theories and not everyone in the room was in agreement. At the same table sat a very quiet young woman, Tatijana, absent-mindedly smoking, even while her eyes showed intense concentration. Her colleague was so overpowering that she never got a word in edgeways, but when he left the room for a while she spoke quickly and urgently.

'Predrag and I are not in agreement on many things,' she almost whispered. 'I think this war is a disaster for Serbia and all Yugoslav people.'

Her worst fear was civil war in Serbia, Serb against Serb, for there were plenty of people opposed to Milošević, but with less and less peaceful means of acting against him.

Milošević has the remnants of the Yugoslav People's Army (JLA) on his side, as well as the Serbian police, and demonstrations have been broken up with force. Worse than that: opposition academics, writers and journalists have been persecuted and sacked from their jobs – just as they have been in Croatia under Tudjman. Petitions signed by thousands of citizens demanding the resignation of Milošević have been ignored, and people are getting desperate.

'I think we will have civil war in Serbia,' said Tatijana, shaking her head, and I wished we could have talked more. But Predrag was back, beaming with righteous satisfaction.

'Let me take you to the refugee office,' Predrag volunteered. 'There you can see for yourself how our people have suffered in Bosnia and Croatia. Talk to them.' It was an opportunity too good to be missed, and I reluctantly said goodbye to Tatijana.

We set off into the afternoon sunshine, past busy shoppers and languid office workers eating sandwiches around the fountain on Trg Republike, a monumental square in the heart of the city. I hurried to keep up with my guide, who walked through the crowd as fast as he talked.

Soon we were climbing the creaking stairs of an old apartment block and thick wooden doors opened up into a clutter of plastic sacks full of clothing, and anxious-looking women and children. The atmosphere was one of subdued busyness, with hushed conversations and several telephones ringing at the same time. People called to each other from different offices, while others were clearly waiting for something to happen.

My introduction to the busy workers here was the same as the one Predrag had given me at the PEN office, only here I was welcomed with a little more circumspection.

'Please,' said one man, 'report the truth when you come to write about us.'

But which truth should I write of? The pro-Milošević Serbian truth or the anti-Milošević Serbian truth? Not to mention the truths of all the other Yugoslav peoples, each with their own insistent version.

What I really wanted was to speak directly with some genuine refugees, and let them tell me of their experiences in their own words. To this end two women from Sarajevo were invited to join us. Both had recently fled the city and, via Predrag translating, they described how they had been forced to leave their homes and all their possessions.

'Why is your country against us?' asked one of the women.

But before I could think of something to say Predrag had hijacked the conversation and it was impossible to talk further with either of the women.

Another woman and her young son entered the office, and Predrag quickly took them under his arm, nodding with solicitude as he listened to her query. While she talked he turned to me and said, 'You see, another one!' as if she were some kind of trophy. His countenance was that of an official of the refugee office itself and it took some time before the poor woman realised she was talking to the wrong person.

It was hopeless. Predrag was not the medium through which to reach anyone at the refugee office. He simply did not allow anyone to speak for themselves, interpreting their comments to his own ends and distorting my questions beyond recognition. It was clear from the answers that he offered in other people's names that he had not asked what I intended.

Exhausted with the effort of non-communication, I told Predrag that I had had enough for one day and we left.

'You see,' he said outside, 'we are God's people, just like the Jews. We have a destiny and we will survive, no matter how hard anyone tries to destroy us.'

There was nothing more to be gained from the encounter, and we shook hands to say goodbye. His final shot was as perplexing as the rest:

'What the world does not understand is that we Serbs are Orthodox Christians. We want only love. Have a look at our icons. You will see they never portray violent scenes, unlike Catholic art. We are a peace-loving nation.'

Men like Predrag sound dangerously fanatical. However, our overall experience of Serbia, as well as the most cursory reading of the country's twentieth-century history, does make it hard to understand why the West has uniformly condemned Serbia alone. One cannot help wonder whose political interests it serves to encourage a war in the Balkans which could almost certainly have been avoided if the international response to this explosive region had been less inflammatory.

It is not in the interests of the European Community to have this war. It is creating dangerous instability and adding to the already serious differences among EC member states, not to mention those who wish to join it. The spectre of a new economic and political superpower called the United States of Europe, which is giving some in North America the jitters, is a long way from emerging as long as a Balkan war threatens to suck in more and more countries. Not only is it making a cohesive Europe impossible for the time being, it is also chipping away at the already crumbling perception among Europeans that their countries could ever exist as a unified entity of any kind.

By the time the war is over, there will most likely be no faith left whatsoever that Europe can ever be anything but a region of competing nations with shifting economic and political alliances. No one will believe any more in a true community of European states, with a unified currency, let alone a centralised political or defence system. In the meantime, EC member governments cannot even agree on ratifying the Maastricht Treaty.

The 'New Europe' will prove to be an illusion – to the immense relief of the ailing superpower on the other side of the Atlantic. Europe will eat itself and the accelerating trade war between the US and the EC will simply put the nail in its coffin.

I came here full of hope, looking for a forward-looking attitude. But what I found instead was hate and a backward-looking stance. That in itself is bad enough, though merely a disappointment. Far worse is that the experience of travelling in Eastern Europe has cracked one of my fundamental beliefs: that cultures may be different, but people are the same all over the world, with the same human needs and desires, such as for a home, affection, a decent life and freedom to live according to their way.

How can I still say that when I have met so many people who cannot countenance the idea that they have anything in common with people from neighbouring nations, let alone with ones from the other side of the world?

The sins of your forefathers still condemn you in this part of the world. To be sure, the past, especially Eastern Europe's, has not been digested and still festers. Even so, I would have hoped to find some agreement for the basic idea that we have our humanity in common. But that is a vain, impossible suggestion in the East/Central European context.

So if the idea that we all have our humanity in common – which demands a fundamental respect for each other's human rights – does not apply in this part of the world, it certainly cannot have any intrinsic validity.

Must I lose my hope and faith to cynical acceptance? I have always tried to cling to a more positive view, to come to a more open and receptive attitude. Conveying my understanding and joy of other countries through travel writing has been my way of chipping away at prejudice.

Now it seems incredibly naive what I have tried to show: simply a useless attempt to prettify the hard fact of life that people do not tend to like or respect each other. For me this has been the harshest lesson learnt: if people have anything in common, it is their ignorance and prejudice.

Can I travel again and try to share anything from now on? I can't answer that now. I only know that I will need a lot of time to recover my confidence. The most tempting response is to turn my back on it all and retreat into the private world of my relationship with Benoît. Soon we will be living in the lush hills of Wales, far away from any kind of violence or fundamental issues, and perhaps that is best for the time being.

Perhaps I can explore other kinds of writing there, maybe try my hand at fiction, where I can make a world more positive than the one I find. That, at least, would be a new creative challenge and not complete defeat: a new direction rather than capitulation and total loss of faith.

Those were the words I wrote in my diary after the experience of Belgrade and Predrag, the cumulative response to this journey that had been developing for many weeks. I felt it growing inside me, like a cancer, suffocating my mind and spirit as it spread.

When the Berlin Wall came down I had thought it was the beginning of a new era, where the future would be more important than the past, where potential for new ways of thinking would be more powerful than lazy, received ideas. I was looking for what Europeans could have in common, especially among young people, who might share a similar excitement about a new culture untainted by past hatreds. I did this because I thought of myself as European. Now I no longer knew.

As long ago as 1953, the visionary Polish writer Czesław Miłosz wrote that 'it is saddening to say goodbye to one's dreams of a federation of equal nations, of a United States of Europe in which differing languages and differing cultures would have equal status.' I should have read his book before I left England – only I would not have believed it true for the 1990s. With hindsight, I might say that I went in search of justification for my beliefs and instead found reality, which did not fit. It seems so obvious now, but it wasn't before.

Benoît is the kind of person who harbours no hope. He is a nihilist, an attitude I have always found totally unacceptable because it goes against my naively hopeful nature. Perhaps that is one of the reasons he enjoys my company: he can experience hope vicariously. Yet if you give up hope you need never despair again, which almost seems an attractive state of being in that context, if only it were not so defeatist. Even in the profound state of disillusion I find myself in, I cannot bring myself to be without hope or expectations altogether. I am too stubborn and competitive for that. However, even I have to give up when faced with the indisputable.

So what makes the idea of a united Europe particularly impossible in Central and Eastern Europe? First must be the undigested past that has not been openly discussed and laid to rest, which makes looking ahead very difficult. Second, the repression of the past forty-five years has led to a paralysing mixture of apathy and conformism on the one hand, and hatred and mistrust on the other.

Third, there is no sense of unity, even among the former Eastern Bloc countries, so how can they feel they have anything in common with capitalist, Western Europe? Travel was severely restricted before 1989 and, for different reasons, still is. Therefore the majority of people have little experience of foreign countries. Ignorant prejudice has had few opportunities of being softened by the experience of travel and cultural exchange, and nationalism and racism have not been discredited as they are in the West, though both persist even there. (A friend in her seventies told me that the popular idea in England that Mediterranean people are unclean only subsided with the growth of tourism after the Second World War.) Furthermore, at no time in European history has there been a tradition or actual state of unity, so why should it be possible now?

Add to these points the profound disillusion of what the fall of communism has brought, in particular the extreme economic hardship, and there is little good faith left for sharing dreams of a united Europe of any kind. In fact, that is the last subject on anyone's mind. Mere survival takes up enough time. So it seems I set myself up for a fall: I tried to escape history and only found myself face to face with it in Eastern Europe.

Finally, it is probably true to say that nations are not on some pre-destined curve of evolution, eventually leading them to the highest form of civilisation, generally considered in the West to be democracy. Rather, the natural state of being is one dominated by violence, and those in democratic countries are simply very lucky to be living during an era that guarantees them relative freedom and prosperity. However, that state is most likely temporary in the wider scale of history, and proves nothing about the superiority of those enjoying it.

Recent wars, initiated by Western countries, such as the Falklands War and Gulf War, show that democratic societies are not above acts of barbarity when their interests are threatened, be they relating to national security, power assertion or greed. Thus, if more wars do ignite in Eastern Europe and the former Soviet Union, there is no reason to think this is because the people are somehow less cultivated in the higher forms of political and social development. What seems to be unnatural for people the world over is civilisation and, time and again, they remain capable of proving this at the slightest encouragement. No country should therefore consider itself above such primitive things as war.

Benoît's reaction to my crisis was to suggest that my focus was too wide. How can anyone understand such concepts as whether or not there is such a person as a European, or whether or not we should or could believe that, if nothing else, we have our humanity in common? Better stick to smaller scales and relate what you actually see and experience, without trying to understand or come to general conclusions – to concentrate on the specific, on actual people and places. Telling a good story alone is worth doing. Perhaps he is right, and Serbia certainly was the most fertile place for meeting people.

'MY HOUSE IS YOURS!'

It was time to leave Belgrade behind, and it was time to leave the Danube as well. We had been following her for almost a month, cycling close to 600 kilometres since Bratislava, but a new guide now beckoned, namely the Morava. It was confusing having two rivers on this journey with the same name, but there it was. This was the Serbian Morava, which joins the Danube near Smederevo and rises in the eastern mountains of Kosovo, almost 400 kilometres further south.

If we had continued east along the Danube, we would soon have come to the watershed of the Iron Gate, and the last stretch of the river leading to the Black Sea – a major trade route since time began, but not the one we were following. Mind you, by now I hardly felt that we were following the historic amber either, so faint had its trail become. The reason for this was obvious enough: archaeological research and field work is very limited when it comes to the Baltic–Aegean route for amber, since it is the oldest of the lot. Probably in use well over a thousand years before the birth of Christ, its secrets are much harder to unveil and, the further south we were travelling, the further away we were getting from later amber trade routes, that overlapped with the earliest one and left more evidence. All I had to go by, from now on, were the educated guesses of historians, who believe the natural route to the Aegean would have been along river valleys offering easy travelling.

Thus we turned due south, to follow a valley washed through the increasingly hilly landscape of southern Serbia, and leading us almost to the borders of Yugoslav Macedonia, where the serious mountains begin. Its capital city, Skopje, is surrounded by at least seven peaks that range between 1,401 and 2,548 metres high, and I dreaded to think how we would get there on the bikes.

For the time being, however, the cycling was easy along quiet country roads of the Morava valley, and for long stretches we cruised at an athletic 25 kilometres per hour. My leg muscles were as tough as they were ever going to get by now, and I enjoyed pushing the pace for short distances. I was never going to be able to keep up with Benoît's potential speed, but at least I could surprise him now and then, and we even raced each other on the occasional uphill sections.

How different to when we first set off, when every incline was agony and Benoît's nonchalant waiting at the top of the hills had infuriated me.

'Don't look so bloody relaxed,' I used to snap.

Now the joy of being fit and in complete control of the bicycle was one of the greatest pleasures. To cruise with ease, to have my body and machine moving in complete harmony was very satisfying, and I enjoyed the admiring looks of the occasional tractor driver as we overtook him. I even showed off a bit, taking a swig from my water-bottle without slowing down or fumbling for it. These were some of the happiest hours.

Every now and then suckling pigs being roasted by the roadside tempted us to break our journey. Delicious-looking crackling glistened in the sun and the smell of cooking meat was wonderful. But, alas, we were so keen to keep moving that we never stopped and, by the time we started looking for somewhere to stay, there were no more roasting spits to be seen.

We reached the town of Svetozarevo by late afternoon, which, however, only had a luxury hotel to stay in. It seemed odd to find only a large hotel in this otherwise unremarkable place, but the town was directly off the motorway heading towards Greece, and many tourist buses stopped here, if they stopped at all. The hotel lobby was all marble and pot plants and the receptionist eyed me with disdain as I peeled off my grubby cycling gloves. Rooms were no less than 150 DM per night, and there was no negotiating.

What to do? Even two friendly policemen could recommend no alternative, so we decided to continue cycling instead. It was getting late and if we were going to camp rough once more, we needed to find a quiet spot, where we would attract the least attention – the main worry always that the bikes might get stolen during the night. We had excellent locks, and usually found a railing or small tree to lock the bikes to, but with such fancy machines there was always a chance that someone would try to carry off whatever he could. (It reminded me of my last journey, when my greatest worry was the donkey getting stolen during the night.)

Benoît was unhappy at the prospect of pitching the tent just anywhere, especially because he was handicapped by having contact lenses. At the very least he needed clean water to wash his hands and, being a city boy through and through, the prospect of roughing it appealed to him even less than camping had in the first place. But, as I saw it, there was no choice, and he dutifully followed me on to a dirt track leading into some fields.

The path led to an abandoned tip, where stagnant pools of water surrounded lumpy waste-ground. It was not very attractive, but it was secluded, and I decided we would stay. The response I got was sullen, to say the least, but I busied on with getting the tent out, and there was nothing for it but to help me. Unfortunately the ground was hard as concrete and not a single pin could be sunk to hold up the tent.

'This is impossible!' huffed Benoît, and I had to agree with him.

So we packed up and cycled off once more, this time the roles reversed as I sunk into despondency and Benoît perked up with the prospect of finding some other kind of accommodation after all.

The nearest place was a small town called Ćuprija, which brought the distance covered in one day to a record 100 kilometres and we arrived at dusk, tired and with not very good prospects for a bed. Again close to the motorway, the only hotel was said to be very expensive, so we did not bother trying to find it. Instead we asked around for a guest house and, to our relief, were directed to a place near the edge of town.

Ćuprija nestles on the banks of the Morava, and its single main street was busy with the daily *korso*, where a string of cafés, shops and a pool hall were the central focus. Teenage girls and boys ignored each other in excited packs, while the older people were strolling the length of the high street or gossiping in doorways. We enjoyed moving slowly among the leisurely flow, and almost forgot that we had nowhere to stay that night.

The guest house turned out to be above an immaculate new restaurant, whose interior was all polished wood and pink tablecloths, while outside a fresh lawn and landscaped garden was tastefully laid out around a marble patio. Clearly it had never had our kind of custom in mind, but the war-redundant staff were so pleased to see us that we were welcomed with free glasses of *rakija*, the local spirit.

Meanwhile, the neighbourhood's boys had spotted us and came to inspect our bikes. I could see them trying to calculate how many gears we had from the number of front chainwheels and rear sprockets, and I proudly told them it was twenty-one.

'Where are you from?' asked the only one who could speak English, and soon we were into conversation about where we were from and what we were doing here. He was called Jovan, a tall and handsome eighteen-year-old, with sensuous features and intelligent brown eyes. Unlike the others, he exuded calm self-assurance, and when I told him we were looking for somewhere to stay, he immediately suggested we sleep at his parents' house.

'Won't they mind?' I asked cautiously, but he insisted it would be all right, and hurried off to ask permission to bring us home. Within minutes he was back.

'My father says it is all right. You may come,' he said, gallantly wheeling my bicycle, as Benoît and I followed.

'Welcome to my house!' said Jovan's father, coming to greet us on the garden path. He was a stocky man with a broad face and a huge smile that seemed to spread from ear to ear. His busy eyebrows curled up like pointed sabres, and his meaty hand clasped mine in an iron grip.

Before we knew it we were sitting on a plush sofa, drinking yet more *rakija*, and slightly dazed by the sudden turn in our fortune. It was only a few hours ago that we had been trying to put our tent up in an abandoned rubbish tip. Yet here we were, feeling slightly uncomfortable in our sweaty cycling pants on Mr Celebić's nice sofa – Miša to us – and wondering how soon we could politely ask where we could wash and change into something more suitable.

Miša was a picture-book patriarch: a powerful presence, who liked to clip his fine son playfully around the ear; he was a pasha in his family kingdom, and enjoyed nothing more than to entertain guests.

'My house is yours! he announced. 'You may stay as long as you wish – a month, a year, it is all right.' He beamed.

His wife arrived, and greeted us with friendly handshakes – as if it were perfectly normal to see us in her sitting-room – while Miša went to check his wine bottles.

'What would you like to drink?' he asked. 'Red wine, white wine or beer?'

But before we had a chance to answer, he said, 'You will have red wine.' He was the master of ceremonies, and everyone took their cue from him.

'I make the wine myself, in my own vineyard,' he told us, and we dutifully admired it, which was easy, because it was excellent.

'Making wine is like a love affair . . . You must cherish the vines every day, and then, at last, you will harvest them at just the right moment, and then you must watch the barrels . . . It is wonderful!' he breezed. Every day, after his engineering work in the local factory, he spent the remaining daylight hours in his small vineyard.

When we told him that we were cycling from Poland to Greece he was intrigued, and soon we were poring over maps, tracing our route. Jovan was a keen cyclist himself, and could well appreciate our journey, while his father was inspired to recall youthful journeys to Greece. In particular he remembered being confused by Greek road signs to Thessaloníki. Serbian maps traditionally refer to the city as Solun, and the young Miša had never heard of its Greek name. Even today many Serbs and Slav Macedonians refer to the city as Solun, which is enough to give some Greeks an apoplectic fit, and convince them that official recognition of the Macedonian Republic threatens their northern province of Macedonia.

By the time it came to dinner, we felt like we were part of the family. It was as if we had come home. Soon we were eating a delicious meal of *pasulj*, spicy bean and bacon soup, along with home-made bread, olives and cheese, and yet more wonderful wine, and I wondered if I could risk bringing up the war in Bosnia.

'What do you think of Milošević?' I asked tentatively. 'He is a wonderful man! A good leader. I was a communist before; so was he.'

Jovan glanced at us, as if to say, 'That's *his* opinion,' and Miša caught him.

'My son does not agree, but he is only a teenager and knows nothing. He only thinks he knows better than his father,' he said, with a benign smile.

'But let's not talk politics,' said Jovan diplomatically, and the conversation moved on to more practical things, like the sanctions.

'I have to go to work by bus now,' said Miša, 'to save on petrol. We only get government coupons for twenty litres of petrol a month, and we cannot go far on that.'

Anyone who wanted more petrol had to buy it for hard currency at special stations, or from the Turkish and Greek truck drivers, who delivered fuel to anyone who could pay. We saw them unloading everything from huge barrels to plastic gallon jugs at restaurants, hotels and private homes all along our route through Serbia. The Black Market is doing a roaring trade, and not just in Serbia either, but throughout Eastern Europe.

The trouble was that most ordinary people could not afford to buy extra petrol. Miša was earning a good salary at US$150 per month, which was apparently well above the national average, but he had no access to hard currency in Ćuprija, and with a family of five to keep, there was no spare cash.

They still lived well, however, and there were no recriminations against our governments. This was not a family that took politics personally, and Miša's assertion that he had been a communist was said in a tone that implied club membership rather than ideological commitment. He could just as well have told me he used to belong to the local football team, though I could tell that his sharp wit hid greater depths than he was prepared to let on. I suspect he did not wish to lower the tone of the occasion − it was part of being a good host.

Jovan was on summer holiday before his last year at school, so he had plenty of time to show us around, and we were persuaded to stay another night. There was one place in particular that they all agreed we should see: Ravanica, one of the most famous Serb Orthodox monasteries. It was just 10 kilometres away, and Miša generously let Jovan borrow his car to take us there.

Ravanica was built in the late fourteenth century, and represents the ultimate style of Serb Orthodox art and architecture before the Turks brought Serbia's Golden Age to a violent end at the Battle of Kosovo, in 1389. It was a terrible defeat, at which Prince Lazar, the last of the Nemanjić dynasty, was killed, and almost the entire Serbian nobility with him. In one fell swoop the Turks destroyed what was one of the most sophisticated and glamorous European kingdoms of the Middle Ages and, what the Hungarians had to endure for 150 years, the Serbs had to suffer for almost five hundred.

The Battle of Kosovo is therefore one of the most potent stories of the country's mythology, and serves to remind Serbians today of the proud heritage they are fighting for. By a strange twist of logic, the historic defeat is the basis on which nationalist Serbs claim the right to leadership in the Yugoslav region. It is celebrated as the most glorious moment in their history, when Serbia made its greatest sacrifice against the Ottoman invasion of Europe. Add to this the ghastly losses of the First and Second World Wars, and nationalists see themselves as having a God-given right to hegemony.

Countless songs, poems and novels take their themes from that long-gone era, and the tragic figure of Prince Lazar features often. It is said that he gathered an army of almost 100,000 men for the final showdown, leading them into battle on the 28th June 1389. But fortune was against his army, and Lazar was decapitated in revenge for the death of Sultan Murad I, who had been killed in the fighting.

The 28th of June is a highly charged date. Not only was the Battle of Kosovo fought then, but the Archduke, Franz Ferdinand, was assassinated on that day in 1914, and it was also the date President Milošević chose to stage his most blatant nationalist celebrations in Kosovo's regional capital of Priština, in 1989. Also in that year, he had the bones of Prince Lazar returned to Ravanica, which was built by him and was his original resting place before his remains were moved north by Serb loyalists.

At this hallowed place we now arrived, and Jovan showed us its architectural highlights with obvious pride. Most of the original fortification and monastery buildings were destroyed long ago, but the church still stands, built in gorgeous shades of cinnamon stone, placed to give a stripy effect, and topped by four cupolas surrounding a central dome. It is a small, compact structure, with beautiful sculpted arches around the exterior, similar to the simple elegance of Romanesque or Norman churches.

Inside, the dark interior was divided into two main areas, quite unlike any Western church. Instead of the familiar nave and transept, designed in a cross fashion, there were two chambers of similar proportions, each about the size of a chapel, except that the main worshipping area of the church was covered by the high central dome, which gave it a very spacious feeling. There were no chairs or stalls, as the congregation stands in Serb Orthodox churches, and the sanctuary, which would normally be behind an alter, was entirely screened from view by an iconostasis (a kind of panel) covered with tiers of gold-leaf icons from floor to ceiling. To the left and right of the 'nave', there were semi-circular 'transepts', where the walls were covered in faded frescos.

It was unlike anything I had ever seen – my first Orthodox church – and we stood in dumb admiration. A priest in long black gown and flowing beard was performing a private ceremony for a young couple at an altar in the entrance hall, and we watched fascinated by his unfamiliar ritual. Meanwhile, a wizened old nun came to sell us trinkets, and we dutifully bought a commemorative postcard.

A small religious community still lives at Ravanica, and near the church stands their home, a magnificent traditional farmhouse of oak beams and whitewashed walls. The location is lovely: set in a lush clearing on the wooded slope of the local hills, where a sparkling spring bubbles up from the depths of a cave behind the monastery, giving life to their vegetable garden and animal pastures. It is said to produce water with miraculous healing powers, and a small stream by the roadside has a constant queue of pilgrims and villagers waiting to fill their containers.

In the evening, Jovan took us to join the local *korso*, and we strolled along the high street as if we had done it all our lives. There was a small military barracks here, and there were quite a few soldiers about as well. Jovan knew many of them, since they were local boys in training, and he stopped often for banter. It was only a year before he would have to go himself: military service was obligatory. He could get no passport before he had done his duty and, although he did not mind going, he was sad that he would not be able to visit us in England for a long time – perhaps never.

I tried to imagine him as one of the soldiers fighting in Bosnia. Would this mild-mannered boy be turned into a killer and learn to commit atrocities, I wondered. I could not imagine it, and I am sure he could not either, but he did know that his future was threatened, and it made him more serious than he should have been. Every time he walked past the barracks he was reminded that he was not just going to do military service, but would most likely fight in a real war.

'How come Western Europe wants to be united, but they don't want a united Yugoslavia?' he asked pensively, but I had no answer for him.

By the steep banks of the Morava, he showed us yet another legacy of war in his country. There was a large steel bridge crossing the river, where the main road entered the town. It was built by the communists, he told us. But a little further upriver were the remains of a Turkish bridge, blown up in one of the many battles that have swept the region. Further up still, there were a few stumps of a Roman bridge, which was the first to be built at this point, and must have been on an important trade and military route.

After the Greek colonies and Alexander the Great's Macedonian Empire declined, the Romans ruled large parts of what was Yugoslavia, from the early first century AD onwards. In fact, after the Roman emperor, Diocletian, divided the empire in AD 285, the first eastern capital was located on the Dalmatian coast, by the modern city of Split, and was only later based in Constantinople (Istanbul).

The division of the Roman Empire was the first step towards the great Schism of the Christian world, which culminated in the papal Bull of Excommunication served on the Church of Constantinople in 1053. It is from that long era that the differences between the two oldest traditions of Christian faith and worship grew, the most obvious being the different scripts. And therein also lies the division of the Yugoslav territory into the Catholic west and the Orthodox east, since the Roman dividing line ran straight through its lands, with the western countries being sent missionaries from Rome, while the eastern countries fell under the sway of Byzantine monks, most famously the brothers Cyril and Methodius, credited with the conversion of the Slavs.

The historic river-crossing at Ćuprija also shows that people have been passing this way for at least one millenium – probably much longer – and some of them were undoubtedly carrying amber. The archaeological and scientific research into Bronze Age amber finds in the Aegean is still in its infancy, but chemical analysis has now firmly established that the amber is from the Baltic, and it only remains to prove how it got there.

On our last morning in Ćuprija we shared a traditional breakfast of *slatko*, a kind of cherry conserve washed down by a glass of water, followed by a very heavy cheese flan in thick pastry, called *burek*, eased down by strong black coffee. It was a substantial meal before having to cycle again, but we could hardly refuse.

We said goodbye to Miša and his wife, while Jovan got the bikes out of the garage, and swung on to his own to join us. He had promised to cycle part of the way, to make sure we did not get lost, but mostly to prolong having to part company. In just two days we had become good friends, and we were all sorry that it was time to leave so soon. But it was the last week in July, and we were trying to make it to Greece by early August.

We cycled almost 25 kilometres before Jovan reluctantly turned back, and we waved farewell for a long while, certain that we would not meet another person so generous and friendly between here and the Aegean.

In spite of Jovan's guidance we did manage to get lost and, by the time we found the right road again, it was way past lunchtime and our stomachs were dreaming of *ćevapčići* and a cold beer. Happily the town of Aleksinac offered just such delights, and soon we were sitting in the shade of a local restaurant, waiting for our meal and fending off the local money-changers.

It was a very hot afternoon and, after a few beers, we were in leisurely mood and decided to try our luck with the local campsite, marked on our map. It was another of the motel-campsites close to the motorway, and to our surprise we were allowed to stay for a reasonable price, even though the only customers were obviously refugees. The camping area was completely empty, the homeless living in the motel rooms, and the melancholy atmosphere was underlined by the leaves of the trees, already falling yellow and forming a shifting sea across the lawns.

In the morning we woke to see women sweeping the leaves into great heaps, which were then transferred to a sheet for carrying to the nearby garbage cans. It was as if this futile tidiness was to compensate for the fact that they had nothing to do, and even a few men joined the sweeping. Only the children seemed to be enjoying themselves, diving through the rustling heaps and playing with some very young puppies.

There were at least five puppies and they were endearingly clumsy, falling off their bow legs and sneezing amongst the musty leaves. One of them was braver than the others, and came foraging close to our tent, tail wagging and ears pointed, and I could not resist cuddling him until I remembered that he probably had fleas. Retrieving him was an opportunity for two middle-aged men to come and chat, and they quickly begged us to take the dog. The puppies had been born on the journey from Bosnia, and they had nothing to feed them with. They were sharing their own food with them, mashing up bread and milk, but there was no future for them. At best they would survive as scavenging strays, but most likely they would die.

'We are eighty people here, all from the same village,' said one of the men. 'I had a fine house and work, but now I have nothing. We have lost everything.'

They had no idea if they could ever return to their village. For them, this campsite was a kind of prison to which they had been sentenced indefinitely. They could go nowhere, do nothing, only while away the hours sweeping the lawn.

The gulf between us was oppressive, and we were glad to leave. Our different circumstances were entirely arbitrary, and that was the worst of it: none of us had done anything to deserve our lot.

Meeting Aleksa in the village of Doljevac meant that we got little further the second day after leaving Ćuprija than we did on the first. He was a wiry little man of about seventy, with a shock of pure-white hair and the wrinkliest face I have ever seen. Yet he was beautiful. His body still moved with lithe agility, and the sharp contrast between his white crew-cut and deeply tanned skin gave him a most striking appearance. He also had a wonderful smile, when his dark eyes twinkled with mischievous winks.

In his right hand was permanently a cigarette, whether lit or not, and he had a regular habit of asking for a light when he could not make his work, which it was obvious had ran out of gas a long time ago. It was as if he was parodying a forgetful old man, when in fact he was nothing of the sort.

It was to him that the local restaurant owner turned when we could find no common language, for Aleksa had spent twenty-five summers selling trinkets all along the Dalmatian and Montenegrin coasts, and he could speak reasonable German, as well as the odd word of French. His favourite phrase was '*comme ci comme ça*', which he used to express anything from 'it's a bit messy in my house' to 'times are uncertain now'.

He loved company and, by the time we had finished our lunch, he had persuaded us to stay at his house, where he boasted he had fourteen rooms for us to choose from. It was just across the street from the restaurant and, it was true, his property consisted of an ancient cottage and a half-finished extension with a great many rooms standing empty.

'I live here all alone,' he said, with a hint of sorrow.

His wife had died two years previously, and her death notice was still attached to his front door. We had seen these bleak announcements everywhere, framed in black, with a small cross and photograph of the deceased. They were not only stuck on doors, but also on church and council notice-boards, and even telegraph poles along the street. Sometimes there were also black flags hanging out of windows, and we had wondered if all these death notices had anything to do with the war. But Aleksa explained that this was merely an Orthodox tradition, and that a person's death is commemorated for a long time after the actual event. The notices normally stay up for several years, and at particular intervals over a decade or so, the departed are remembered and celebrated by special feasts.

'My wife weighed twice as much as me,' he chuckled, and soon we were leafing through faded family albums recalling the seven decades of his life so far. Aleksa hunting pigeons as a boy, Aleksa getting married, the children (a girl and a boy), Aleksa clasped by his huge wife and, his most treasured photograph: the one with the article written about him when he was a successful trader of home-made crafts on the Adriatic coast. The only problem was that the article was in Italian, so he had no idea what it said about him.

'Now there are no more tourists,' he sighed, looking at his sacks full of paper snakes and straw men. His pension was approximately US$30 a month, which was hardly enough for an old man to live on, and he survived by doing odd jobs around the village. He did not eat much, but he did like to smoke at least a packet a day, and he also still loved driving his battered old car. To start it he needed to join two wires under the steering wheel, but then it worked fine, and he took us for a spin around the village.

Doljevac was nothing special – simply a dusty one-street affair that was gradually fusing with a neighbouring village along the same road – but being with Aleksa put a whole different light on things, especially after the *rakija* we drank at his relative's farmhouse.

Talk was of the big summer festival scheduled for the next day, and it was with this that Aleksa persuaded us to stay another day.

'It will be a huge event,' he said, 'there will be hundreds of people coming from all the surrounding villages and you won't be able to move on this street!'

He took us to the local church, where preparations were well under way. It was a very simple version of the Ravanica church, the walls covered in folk-art frescos and the dome a garish blue sprinkled with gold stars. Garlands and plastic flowers were being attached to every space possible, especially around the icons, while outside, in the grassy church-yard, a merry-go-round and mini fairground were being put up. Already the balloon and candyfloss sellers were doing a good trade, and a handful of market stalls were covered in everything from plastic toys to shoes and make-up.

It was going to be a great day, Aleksa assured us, and we looked forward to it. But that was tomorrow. For tonight we simply drove back to his home, where poor Benoît failed to use the hole-in-the-ground toilet. His bowels simply refused to co-operate when faced with a black pit, and I was only glad not to have the same problem, especially since we were not to encounter a standard Western toilet until after the Greek border. (Most public toilets in Serbia are much worse, comprising two raised foot pads over a small hole, which is inevitably blocked.)

The day's festivities began with a great feast at Aleksa's brother's farm, which was conveniently almost next-door to the church, and we arrived to find a large number of relatives already assembled. The brother and his wife were around the same age as our friend, and equally striking, especially the wife. She was a sturdy old woman, almost as broad as she was tall, dressed in traditional working smock and headscarf, but with extraordinary aquamarine blue eyes. In her youth she must have been stunning and, despite her fleshy figure and crumpled skin, she was still beautiful now.

They could not have known that Aleksa was going to bring two strangers, but it made no difference, and we were invited to join the family table without much ado. A large wooden table was prepared on a porch overhung with grapevines, and we sat in the cool shade while the first course was brought out with the wine. First there was home-made cheese and tomatoes, sprinkled with fresh basil, salt and pepper. Then came a delicious vegetable soup with liver dumplings in it, followed by a round of boiled eggs from their own chickens, and aubergine fritters with a salad of tomato and cucumber.

We felt like the main part of the meal must have been served by now, but that was only the beginning. Shortly there arrived huge plates of meat, with a selection of roast chicken legs, sausages, and pork cutlets in breadcrumbs, together with warm bread from their own wood-burning oven, and large plates of stuffed peppers, with a choice of spicy relishes.

It was unbelievable the amount of food that came in a constant stream from the kitchen, where the grandmother and daughter-in-law were preparing each course entirely fresh, never sitting at the table for more than a moment and only snatching the occasional bite, while the rest of us gorged ourselves. It was a wonderful meal that went on for the whole afternoon, only gradually ending with the last few courses of sweets, that began with boiled pears in syrup and ended with huge slices of creamy gâteau.

We felt like we could not possibly eat again for at least a week, and not even *rakija* could help ease the pain. At last the women joined the table, and we thanked them from our hearts for their delicious creations. The agony in our bellies was worth every mouthful and, as the hours passed in lively conversation, we gradually regained mobility.

We got on particularly well with Aleksa's two teenage nephews, who spoke just enough English to make interesting conversations possible, and we decided to go and explore the fair. Loud music had blasted our ears all day, with a brass band and assorted singers next-door, and pop music from the merry-go-round just down the road. It was indeed a lively event, but nothing on the scale that Aleksa had suggested. He had exaggerated wildly to keep us for another night, but we did not blame him for that. I would not have missed this day for anything.

There were perhaps one hundred villagers milling about, mostly children and teenagers, and our escorts thought it was all pretty basic. They lived in the nearby industrial city of Niš and found this provincial fair rather tame: no video games or dangerous rides to go on. We wandered off into the surrounding hills, where Aleksa's brother, their grandfather, owned substantial orchards of cherry, apricot and other fruit, as well as maize fields and cereals. The Morava valley is a rich agricultural region, like almost all of Serbia, and we could well appreciate that trade sanctions would never starve this land.

When we left to return home with Aleksa, we exchanged addresses with the two boys and promised to keep in touch.

'We may be from the Balkans,' said one, 'but we are not barbarians.'

It was an oblique reference to the portrayal of Serbs in the Western media, and I could only reply that a warmer people I have rarely met, anywhere in the world.

5. MACEDONIA

This is the new Eastern Europe – a labyrinth whose winding paths are beyond the comprehension of the most skilled cartographer.

Misha Glenny,
The Rebirth of History, 1993

HOME RUN

The experience of Serbia left us so exhausted that we had no mental energy left. It had been exhilarating and a pleasure, but there was also a lot of information and impressions to digest, and we longed to find ourselves at home already, where a washing-machine and peace awaited.

One of the small details of long journeys that gradually becomes more and more intrusive is the fact that you are stuck with wearing the same two T-shirts and trousers for weeks on end. Rarely can you wash yourself or your clothes as often as you would like to, and the usual wear and tear of being on the move means that you soon look unavoidably scruffy. This is irrelevant in the wilds, but in populated, 'civilised' areas, it does become a little embarrassing.

After travelling for a couple of months, minor inconveniences start to grow into tedious burdens: the daily packing and unpacking of your bags, putting the tent up, always remembering to take toilet paper with you, even the routine of finding somewhere to stay. Familiar questions – like 'How much is the room (campsite)? Do you have hot water?' – become a drag to ask without appearing rudely disinterested and, worst of all, your senses eventually become dull to new impressions. The travel writer, Martin Jordan, once told me that he considered six months the maximum limit for any journey in Latin America. For Europe I would cut that down to two or three, because of the density of cultures and languages.

At any rate, by the time it came to leaving Aleksa we had had enough, our bodies tired and our minds saturated, and I was tempted to get on the next direct train to Greece. But that would have been cheating too much, so we just took a train for the 200 kilometres from Doljevac to Skopje, which was enough to take us out of Serbia and into Macedonia.

We waved goodbye to our friend from the train, and stood squeezed among Serbian peasants on their way to market at the nearest town – no pushing and shoving this time. Later we managed to find seats, and sat with a shy country family dressed in black. The father's weathered hands lay awkwardly on his pressed suit, while his wife and daughter sat stiffly upright, holding alien handbags. None spoke, their faces an immutable blank until they got off, a few stops later, when funeral tears flowed on the platform. We sat alone after that, the sad atmosphere still lingering in the compartment, and we watched Serbia recede in silence.

As we trundled slowly south, the passing scenery presented ox-drawn carts and people making hay, while the landscape gradually became mountainous and dry. The rich pastures of northern and central Serbia were giving way to muted tones of silvery green and sun-dried brown. Prickly shrubs and bushes covered rocky hills, where goats and sheep flocked nibbling by the railway tracks. Occasionally we saw a slender minaret rising above a village, and caught our first glimpse of Moslem skull-caps.

Before reaching Macedonia, the train was more or less following the provincial border with Kosovo, and there were obviously quite a few Moslems living on the Serbian side as well. In fact, Aleksa had strongly urged us to take the train to Skopje, not just because of the increasingly hilly landscape, but also because of 'those Albanians', though I suspect he had never met any personally. But he was convinced they were all bandits, and by this stage we were happy to use his opinion to justify our choice of transport. Serbia had already been rich enough for us, and much time would be needed to absorb even the small portion we had been served.

What had once been a federal demarcation was now an international border – even if it was not yet recognised by the European Community – and our passports were duly checked on entering the new Republic of Macedonia, with its own, freshly printed currency. In fact, we were entering a State in limbo, a country whose identity few except the 'Macedonians' appeared to be taking seriously, much less the historic and cultural basis it claimed for its right to exist.

Even linguistically any discussion of the subject falters, for according to the Greek government, Macedonians are the Greeks living in their northern province of Macedonia. For the fledgling republican government, however, Macedonians are the Slavs living under their jurisdiction. Serbian nationalists, on the other hand, claim Macedonians are nothing more than Serbs, who were wrongly given republic status by Tito, while their Bulgarian counterparts insist they are really Bulgarians. It is therefore impossible to use the word without specifying who exactly one is referring to and, either way, one cannot avoid causing offence. Certain is, however, that both ethnic Slav and Greek Macedonians cannot imagine calling themselves anything other than 'Macedonians'. Yet neither group feels fraternal about the other.

The historic basis for the new Macedonian State is controversial, to say the least. The original people to settle the northern Aegean were Thracians and Greeks. Their influence, however, did not spread far north of the coastal area. Alexander the Great's Macedonian Empire certainly did, encompassing not only modern Slavic Macedonia, but also parts of Albania and western Bulgaria, in a huge domain that stretched from Greece to Egypt and Persia. The trouble is, modern Greek and Slav historians disagree on whether or not Alexander was, in fact, Greek. According to the Greek orator, Demosthenes, the emperor's father was a 'barbarian'.

The Macedonian region has also been ruled by the Romans, Byzantines, Turks, Bulgarians and Serbians and, not surprisingly, has been at the heart of many wars. The last of these were the First and Second Balkan Wars, fought early this century. The first war involved an alliance of Serbia, Bulgaria and Greece against Turkey. The second involved a conflict over territorial gains between the victorious allies, which resulted in Bulgaria losing out to Serbia and Greece.

Thus all these countries can justify claims on Macedonia to varying degrees, but it is the Greeks for whom the very name goes to the heart of their national pride. Add to this the Slav tendency to call their second city Solun instead of Thessaloniki, and Greek nationalists firmly believe that recognition of the Republic of Macedonia is the first step to another territorial war. Of course their Slav neighbours are certain the threat comes from the other side. Why else deny their right to exist?

For us these complexities were not only beyond our understanding, but we could also not help feeling the whole issue was a little mad. Even Benoît's Quebecois heart could not identify with the Macedonian problem, and I innocently asked someone in Skopje why they could not simply change their name to something else. After all, what's in a name? 'Why don't you call yourself Fred, then?' was the pert reply.

No wonder the Balkans has a reputation for convoluted problems and violence! It would take years of study to come to an informed opinion on the region and, as Benoît had already pointed out, it was better for me to stick to smaller scales. By now I was happy to agree with him, though the frustration of knowing I was only scratching the surface of things never disappeared entirely.

At first glance Skopje felt like a concrete city, with dusty gashes for roads, and open spaces that felt more like wasteland than city squares. No wonder either, when you realise that this is a city that has risen out of the rubble of one of the region's worst earthquakes. On 26 June 1963 Skopje was devastated, and what you see today is a strange mix of modern, communist architecture and the remains of the ancient Turkish quarter, sprawling underneath a hilltop mosque.

Old and new are divided by the cloudy waters of the Vardar River, which gives welcome relief with its leafy banks and municipal greenery, where cool paths shade ambling pedestrians and the occasional kiosk. The city is not large, and it is hard to conceive that Skopje could ever be more than a provincial backwater, much less a capital.

When we went to the local telephone exchange to make an international call, the operator was unable to get a connection. The system was relatively new, but unfortunately did not seem to work properly, and he suggested we try again tomorrow.

'How can this be an independent country?' snorted Benoît. 'They can't even make their phones work.'

On the other hand, working telephones were not so common in many East European countries, especially not for long-distance calls.

Out of Serbia, we were lucky enough to find the local campsite running normally, though we were still the only foreign visitors. Tourism has never been big in Macedonia, and the Third Balkan War was keeping away the usual trickle of tourists heading south to Greece. Nevertheless, prices were steep, and we paid US$16 for the privilege of putting our tent up. The friendly attendant shook his head in disbelief when we suggested the price was high.

'You are rich,' he insisted. 'I earn US$30 per month working at this campsite, and sometimes I am here twenty-four hours in one stretch.'

It was true. Compared to him we were rich, but I still felt the price was unreasonable, considering the Üröm site had cost less than half as much. However, set in a park near the river and the city centre, it was pleasant enough, and the food at the open-air restaurant was very good.

We set off to explore the city in the glowing light of early evening. People were just beginning to fill the streets, and the main flow was across the stone bridge leading to the labyrinth of narrow streets, where once the bazaar had thrived. Here the scale was much smaller, and the spaciousness of the new city was replaced by an ancient huddle of crooked shops and cafés. Set on a slope, the cobbled alleyways twisted and curled in inviting mystery, each new turn beckoning you to explore what might lie beyond the next corner.

Old men in skull-caps sat in doorways, fingering prayer beads – some made of amber – while young guns stood admiring their reflection in shop windows. In fact, amber is highly prized in the Islamic world: the fragrant pine scent, when warmed, makes it very popular for prayer beads, as well as for pipe mouthpieces and cigarette holders, while traditional faith in its magical healing power is still kept. In the Middle East, I am told, people like to give each other amber necklaces for good luck. The belief that amber can protect you from sickness and evil is not just current among the uneducated either – even the shahs of Persia used to wear a piece of amber to protect them from assassination, though I do not know if the ayatollahs of Iran do the same today.

The girls in the old quarter were dressed in garish, skin-tight dresses, swinging hips accentuated by high heels, and frills caressing doughy cleavages. Their provocative appearance was strangely at odds with the Islamic atmosphere, and there was a whiff of danger that made us feel we would not walk these streets at night.

The oriental feel of the place was underlined by the faces of the people, many of whom had olive skin and thick black hair, and the maze of shops and market stalls combined to make you imagine you were almost in Turkey. In reality it was, of course, nothing of the sort. But Skopje was the first place where the Ottoman past most obviously lingered and the remains of their architecture, such as the mosques and occasional minaret, gave you a strong impression of their presence here. Were it not for the destruction of the last earthquake, that impression would probably be even stronger.

By chance we found a local tour agency and went inside to browse around. The staff were so amazed to see us that we were promptly invited to eat ice-cream with them.

'What are you doing here?' they asked. 'We have only had four customers in the last month! You must stay, we have many beautiful monasteries you can visit in the mountains.'

'If only we had time,' we declined.

Truthfully, it was more a matter of not wanting to. At this stage we had only the end of our journey in sight, and Macedonia could not keep us. The mountains towering over the Vardar plain looked jagged and for-bidding, and a glance at the map showed that only a major highway, punctuated by tunnels, led the way south-east. It was no route for cyclists, and as there seemed to be no small roads to take instead, we set off the next morning to catch a train to Demir Kapija, a tiny village on the Vardar, where the first country road begins to follow the river towards Greece. The village was almost 100 kilometres further on, just beyond the worst of the mountains, and secretly I was relieved.

Apart from the tobacco fields on the plain, the landscape beyond Skopje took on a distinctly Greek aspect – or at least how we imagined it should be. Barren hills stood littered with bone-white rocks and boulders, treeless, except in the nooks and crannies along occasional streams. Wind-bent thorny bushes huddled on the lower slopes, and there seemed to be hardly any villages at all. It was an empty land, battered by the extreme elements of burning summers and bitterly cold winters.

Next to the railway track, the Vardar River tumbled violently south-east, compressed into a rapid current by the ancient rock, and the only people we did see were fishermen trying to catch a meal from the swirling waters. It seemed like a dismal occupation to us, but Macedonia is desperately poor, and self-reliant food gathering is common practice.

Demir Kapija turned out to be just a small place, where donkey-drawn carts bumped over dirt tracks, and our arrival was enough to bring out the local policeman. At first he merely watched us mounting our gear back on to the bicycles, but then could not resist detaining us after all.

'Passports!' he demanded, his chest swelling with self-importance, and quickly a friend had joined him to inspect our documents. Together they fingered the pages like nosy schoolboys, and Benoît, who hates officialdom at the best of time, bristled with hostility. Happily their attention was all on the exotic passports, and we were released without trouble.

Just past the village, the river finally squeezed between the last outcrops of the Macedonian mountains, through a dramatic gorge, drawn together like giant curtains. Only the width of the river let you glimpse the other side, where a spacious valley opened up into the distance. Soon the river would lead us out on to the Greek plain and the shores of the Aegean Sea and the excitement of it sent us flying down the valley.

It was going to be more or less downhill from now on and, with the wind in our backs, the cycling was exhilarating. Almost without effort we shot ahead, our minds free to enjoy the softening contours of the landscape and dream about the approaching sea. Near our feet, the seemingly barren roadside was alive with phallic cactus plants in full yellow bloom, and delicate pink flowers sprinkled the ground. Far below, the speeding river rushed ahead in a deep furrow, worked into a broad channel by the time we reached the last town before the border.

Gevgelija was our last chance to get rid of our Macedonian currency, called *denar* instead of dinar, in order to distinguish it from the old Yugoslav currency, but equally useless beyond its borders. We ordered a sumptuous meal of kebabs in the best restaurant we could find, and recklessly drank a bottle of wine in the hot afternoon sun. It must have been almost 40 degrees when we set off once more, and we crossed the border in an alcoholic haze.

A few kilometres into Greece we stopped again to savour our return to a more familiar Europe. Benoît was delighted to drink his first bottle of Greek retsina (half a litre this time!), while I drooled over a delicious traditional salad with feta cheese, black olives, crisp lettuce and tomatoes. I don't know if it was the wine or the knowledge that we had almost made it to the end of our journey, but a deep sense of satisfaction set in. Nothing could bother us now. Tomorrow we would reach the end of the amber trail and see the sea!

I had almost forgotten about our amber trail – so much had happened to divert my attention from it over past weeks. Not only that, but the lack of tangible landmarks had made it fade into the background of our journey. I had simply accepted the general consensus for the correct route for amber travelling from the Baltic to the Aegean, and thought no more about it, though I knew dissenting voices have argued that amber might have come via Germany and Italy, and then by sea, or even by sea altogether.

The richest amber find in Greece was discovered at Kakovatos, on the west coast of the Peloponnese, which leads some to believe that amber must have arrived by sea and not by land. Rather than being taken more or less directly south, they argue that Baltic amber was taken to Germany, over the Alps to the Italian coast, and from thence by ship to Greece. The theory is further strengthened by the similarity of craftsmanship between the amber beads found at Kakovatos, and those found in south German hoards.

Most likely different routes were taken at different times in history. On the other hand, the idea that we might have followed a non-existent historic route added an attractive irony to my project. After all, my search for a unified European culture had been in vain, perhaps as elusive as the magic of amber itself.

If amber did travel along our route, however, people would have carried it on a path where now the motorway lies. This road was the most obvious link with the past, probably built over a track people have used from time immemorial. I tried to picture the prehistoric scene, even while modern traffic was overtaking us, tried to imagine the huge time span of thousands of years, but all I could think of was that we were simply more ants scuttling past on a vastly old earth, which made all human history seem tiny.

The only certainty is that Baltic amber *did* reach the Aegean as early as 2600–2000 BC, where it was used by the Minoan culture on Crete. This early European civilisation was also one of the great seafaring nations of history, so they might well have sent ships all the way to the Baltic. Once their hegemony declined, from 1400 BC onwards, the Mycenaean civilisation, based in the Peloponnese, took over. They too loved amber, as we know from their tombs.

Strictly speaking, therefore, we could have extended our journey all the way to southern Greece or the island of Crete. But that would have taken the historical basis of our journey too far beyond the confines of Eastern Europe, which was the main focus of this project. Greece deserves a journey in its own right anyway, and what little we saw certainly made us want to return.

The first town we came to was lined with small hotels, and soon we were resting on pristine linen, stripy shadows cast over the room by wooden shutters on the windows, and a gentle breeze coming in from the balcony. We had arrived during the dead hours of a Greek afternoon, and almost no sounds disturbed the silence. But for us, the hotel was empty anyway, as were all the others, and even the dogs were asleep.

Later the hotelier complained bitterly that the Yugoslav war had killed his business. Ever since the main flow of tourists no longer arrived overland, from the north, his hotel had stood virtually unused, and that just when he had finished building a luxury hotel across the street. It was an economic disaster for the whole town.

It was only another 60 kilometres to Thessaloníki and, fresh and sober the next morning, we set off for our last day of cycling. The shimmering horizon hovered tantalisingly, like a distant sea, and we urged our legs into one final effort. Progress was difficult, however, because the great Macedonian plain was being blasted by wind coming off the Aegean, and an invisible force pushed against us for most of the way. Nearing the city, the wind turned to batter us from the side, almost ripping the handlebars out of my grip, and turning the last 20 kilometres into an absolute misery.

The wind blew so hard that my ears rang maddeningly, and dust flew constantly in our faces. Huge lorries almost pushed us off balance in the wake of their turbulence, and there were times when I thought I would rather walk than fight on like this. Every pedal stroke was hell, our spirits only slightly raised when we finally passed the metropolitan sign for the city. Only a few kilometres now . . .

I crossed a railway track and suddenly heard loud swearing behind me: 'I don't believe this! I've got a puncture!'

It was impossible. He must be joking, I thought, but looked back anyway. Sure enough, Benoît *did* have a puncture. 'Never take railway tracks too fast, because the strain on your back tyre might make it burst.' How often had he told me that! Yet now, after almost 2,000 kilometres of cycling, on our last day, almost on our last kilometre, he had done just that: the weight of the panniers had smacked his back wheel on to the ground too hard, and the inner tube had promptly burst. Well, at least we had not carried our spares entirely for nothing.

The look on Benoît's face made me restrain my laugh, but he lost his temper anyway. Before I knew it, he was ripping the panniers off the back

wheel, kicking and shouting, and pounding the tangled heap in a scream-
ing rage. Meanwhile a constant stream of traffic was passing by, and one
driver wagged his finger out of the window, as if to say: 'Temper,
temper'. Luckily his gesture went unnoticed, because Benoît would
surely have attacked the car as well. The tantrum did not last long,
though, and he laughed about it soon enough. Changing the wheel was
not difficult, only time-consuming, and we arrived in downtown Thessaloníki only marginally later than expected.

The city's waterfront curved in an attractive arc, with fine turn-of-the-
century hotels and apartment blocks lining a spacious promenade. Stone
steps, dotted with tiny molluscs and slippery with seaweed, led down into
the waves, and what a thrill it was to put our bare feet into the sea at last! A
port was not the ideal place to do it, but I could not have cared less.
Pelicans bobbed among squawking seagulls, even here, and the brisk sea
air was a pleasure now. We had made it from the Baltic to the Aegean in
just two months, yet the journey had felt much longer than that, and we
gazed out to sea in a dazed stupor.

Personally, I felt I had chased an idea that turned out to be an illusion,
and I mourned the loss of it. There were no regrets – at least not really. I
was glad to have found the true character of Europe, though I could not
shake off the sadness of it yet. The encounter was a bruising experience,
but also exciting and joyous. I could not love Europe less because I had
discovered a profoundly disturbed side, only with less expectation. The
relationship was bound to continue, though I intended to keep the lid on
the darker side firmly shut from now on. One look was enough.

Having found a hotel, we spent a leisurely afternoon walking the streets
of this not unattractive city. A constant breeze lifted the heat and traffic
fumes above our heads and, though hardly a tourist town, there were
some beautiful churches. The Agia Sophia, dating from the eighth
century, and built in imitation of its famous namesake in Istanbul, was a
cool and elegant haven. A baptism was just taking place when we entered
the church, and we were permitted to watch the ceremony from a
distance.

The priest was an immensely hairy man, with long grey wisps sprouting
from his face and neck, and a knot of traditionally uncut hair above his
collar. Rolled up cassock sleeves revealed forearms any wrestler would
have been proud of, and his workman-like movements rather clashed

with his office. He circled the font several times, followed by the father of the child, both intoning prayers throughout. Meanwhile, a young girl, of about two, was stripped naked by her mother, and handed to the priest, who must have been a terrifying sight for her.

All the while, blinding white light flooded the scene for the benefit of a photographer, and the poor child screamed in protest when she was three times bodily submerged in water, once for each invocation of the Holy Trinity, while an assistant punctuated with 'A-ha-men' over a micro-phone. This done, the shivering child was anointed with a special ointment, the priest marking her forehead, eyes, nose, ears, chest, hands and feet, which signified her immediate confirmation into the Orthodox Church. Only then could she be handed back to her mother, who comforted her with a towel, and proceed to dress her in virgin white from top to toe. The child seemed confused and rather shocked. But from today, the celebration of this date would be more important than her birth. And the original experience equally forgotten, I hoped.

Returned to the warming sun, we ambled back to our hotel and packed our bags for the last time. There was no reason to prolong the end and, after one last night of being too hot and savaged by mosquitoes, we cycled to the airport for a flight home. I enjoyed the fact that we were going to the airport under our own steam, and the bikes were loaded on to the plane with no more fuss than they had been stored on the ferry, back at Harwich.

It felt strange to return to familiar things in just a few hours. When we had set off, I had especially wanted to go overland to retain a sense of being within one region: Europe. Now I felt I was returning from very far away – somewhere much too far away to come back by land.

POSTSCRIPT

Since this book was completed, Czecho-Slovakia has dissolved into separate countries: the Czech Republic and Slovakia. The war in Bosnia continues, and there is every chance that it will spread to the Serbian province of Kosovo, where 90 per cent of the population are Moslem Albanians. The former Yugoslav province of Macedonia, which was denied EC recognition as an independent republic because of Greek opposition to the name, has now been recognised as the Former Yugoslav Republic of Macedonia. However, violence could still erupt because of the large Albanian minority, which constitutes up to 40 per cent of the population, and may demand some kind of self-rule. Rioting broke out in the capital, Skopje, shortly after we left.

The drive to nationalist self-determination is also gathering force in western Europe, with Belgium due to have a referendum on the question of independence for its constituent ethnic groups. In Italy, the independence movement for northern Lombardy is gathering pace, and there is increasing pressure for a referendum there too. Meanwhile, the war in Northern Ireland continues, as does the guerrilla fighting by Basque separatists in northern Spain. There is also potential violence brewing in Corsica, where nationalists would like to end French rule. Perhaps East and West Europe are not so different after all.

The nationalist trend is by no means a European one either. Other Western countries are also affected: Canada looks set to lose its largest province, Québec, in the next referendum on secession. Meanwhile, Australian premier, Paul Keating, won the 1993 election with a pledge to hold a referendum regarding his country becoming a republic, no longer a member of the British Commonwealth with the Queen as official Head of State.

APPENDIX

AGENCIES CONSULTED

Cyclists Touring Club, Cotterell House, 69 Meadrow, Godalming, Surrey GU7 3HS.

Expedition Advisory Centre, Royal Geographical Society, 1 Kensington Gore, London SW7 2AR.

PEN, English Centre, 7 Dilke Street, London SW3 4JE.

School of Slavonic and East European Studies, University of London, Senate House, Malet Street, London WC1E 7HU.

South Bank Polytechnic, The Language Centre, 103 Borough Road, London SE1 0AA.

The British Museum Library, London WC1B 3DG.

The Writers' Guild of Great Britain, 430 Edgware Road, London W2 1EH.

University of London Library, Senate House, Malet Street, London WC1.

BIBLIOGRAPHY

Please note: In all cases I have listed the edition used, which is not necessarily the first edition or the one still in print. Other than the books mentioned below, I used a wide variety of British newspaper and magazine articles for my sources, specifically for statistical information.

HISTORIC AMBER

Andrée, K. *Der Bernstein und seine Bedeutung in Natur und Geisteswissenschaften, Kunst und Kunstgewerbe, Technik, Industrie und Handel*, Königsberg, 1937

Beck, C. & Shennan, S. *Amber in Prehistoric Britain*, Oxford, Oxbow Books, 1991

Bezecky, T. 'Roman amphorae from the amber route in western Pannonia', *British Archaeological Report*, 1987

Buffum, W. A. *The Tears of Heliades, or Amber as a Gem*, London, Sampson Low & Co, 1900

Christiansen, E. *The Northern Crusades*, London, Macmillan, 1980

Clark, J. G. D. *Prehistoric Europe: The Economic Basis*, London, Methuen, 1952

East, W. G. *An Historical Geography of Europe*, London, Methuen, 1948

Gimbutas, M. *The Prehistory of Eastern Europe, vol. 1*, Peabody Museum, 1956

Gimbutas, M. *Bronze Age Cultures in Central and Eastern Europe*, The Hague, Mouton & Co, 1965

Grabowska, J. *The Significance of Amber in Polish History*, City of Edinburgh Museums and Art Galleries, 1978

Grabowska, J. *Polish Amber*, Warsaw, Interpress, 1983

Hunger, R. *The Magic of Amber*, London, NAG Press Ltd, 1977

Maccall, W. & Haddow J. G. *Amber: All About It*, Liverpool, Cope & Co, 1891

Milisauskas, S. *European Prehistory*, London, Academic Press, 1978

Navarro, J. M. de 'Prehistoric routes between northern Europe and Italy defined by the amber trade', *The Geographical Journal*, vol LXVI, number 6 (1925)

Renfrew, C. *Problems in European Prehistory*, Edinburgh University Press, 1979

Spekke, A. *The Ancient Amber Routes and the Geographical Discovery of the Eastern Baltic*, Stockholm, M. Goppers, 1957

Sturms, E. 'Der Ostbaltische Bernsteinhandel in der Vorchristlichen Zeit', Jahrbuch des Baltischen Forschungsinstituts, *Commentationes Balticae I*, Bonn, 1953

Tacitus, *The Agricola and the Germania*, London, Penguin Classics, 1970

Wheeler, M. *Rome Beyond the Imperial Frontiers*, London, G. Bell & Sons, 1954
Williamson, G. C. *The Book of Amber*, London, Ernest Benn Ltd, 1932

TRAVEL
Allcock, J. B. & Young, A. *Black Lambs and Grey Falcons, Women Travellers in the Balkans*, Bradford University Research Ltd, 1991
Brook, S. *The Double Eagle*, London, Picador, 1987
Chamberlain, L. *In the Communist Mirror*, London, Faber & Faber, 1990
Dunford, M. & Holland, J. *Yugoslavia: The Rough Guide*, 1986
Durham, M. E. *Through the Lands of the Serb*, London, Edward Arnold, 1904
Fermor, P. L. *A Time of Gifts*, London, Penguin, 1979
Fermor, P. L. *Between the Woods and the Water*, London, Penguin, 1988
Harding, G. *In Another Europe*, London, Hodder & Stoughton, 1990
Humphreys, R. *Czechoslovakia: The Rough Guide*, 1991
MacLean, R. *Stalin's Nose*, London, Flamingo, 1993
Magris, C. *Danube*, London, Collins Harvill, 1991
Richardson, D. & Hebbert, C. *Hungary: The Rough Guide*, 1992
Salter, M. & McLachlan, G. *Poland: The Rough Guide*, 1991
West, R. *Black Lamb and Grey Falcon*, London, Macmillan, 1955
Whittell, G. *Lambada Country*, London, Chapmans, 1992

HISTORY AND ANALYSIS
Birnbaum, H. *Aspects of the Slavic Middle Ages and Slavic Renaissance Culture*, New York, P. Lang, 1991
Castle-Kanerova, M. (ed.) *High Hopes*, London, Virago, 1992
Corrin, C. (ed.) *Superwomen and the Double Burden*, London, Scarlet Press, 1992
Davies, N. *Heart of Europe*, Oxford, OUP, 1991
Dvornik, F. *The Making of Central and Eastern Europe*, London, Polish Research Centre, 1949
Enzensberger, H. M. *Europe, Europe*, London, Picador, 1990
Garton Ash, T. *We the People*, London, Granta, 1990
Garton Ash, T. *The Polish Revolution*, London, Granta, 1991
Garton Ash, T. *The Uses of Adversity*, London, Granta, 1991
Glenny, M. *The Fall of Yugoslavia*, London, Penguin, 1992
Glenny, M. *The Rebirth of History*, London, Penguin, 1993
Miłosz, C. *The Captive Mind*, London, Penguin, 1985
New Europe!, Granta Publications, 30, Winter 1990
Sugar, P. F. *Southeastern Europe under Ottoman Rule,* 1354–1804, London, University of Washington Press, 1977
Sugar, P. F. et al *A History of Hungary*, London, I. B. Tauris & Co, 1990
Thompson, E. A. *A History of Attila and the Huns*, Oxford, OUP, 1948
Ware, T. *The Orthodox Church*, London, Penguin, 1983

LITERATURE

Andrić, I. *The Days of the Consuls*, London, Forest Books, 1992

Esterházy, P. *Helping Verbs of the Heart*, London, Quartet, 1993

Grass, G. *The Tin Drum*, London, Picador, 1989

Grass, G. *Cat and Mouse*, London, Picador, 1989

Grass, G. *Dog Years*, London, Picador, 1989

Grass, G. *The Call of the Toad*, London, Secker, 1992

Gillon, A. & Krzyzanowski L. (eds.) *Introduction to Modern Polish Literature*, London, Rapp & Whiting, 1968

Hesse, H. *Die Morgenlandfahrt*, Frankfurt am Main, Suhrkamp Verlag, 1990

Kafka, F. *The Castle*, London, Minerva, 1992

Keneally, T. *Schindler's Ark*, London, Sceptre, 1991

Kiš, D. *Hourglass*, London, Faber & Faber, 1992

Klíma, I. *Love and Garbage*, London, Penguin, 1991

Kundera, M. *The Unbearable Lightness of Being*, London, Faber & Faber, 1991

Manning, O. *The Balkan Trilogy*, London, Mandarin, 1990

Michener, J. *Poland*, London, Corgi, 1985

Styron, W. *Sophie's Choice*, London, Picador, 1992